Women Administrators

Women Administrators
Challenges in the New Millennium

Dr. B. Madhana Rekha

NEW DAWN PRESS, INC.
USA• UK• INDIA

NEW DAWN PRESS GROUP
Published by New Dawn Press Group
New Dawn Press, Inc., 244 South Randall Rd # 90, Elgin, IL 60123
e-mail: sales@newdawnpress.com
New Dawn Press, 2 Tintern Close, Slough, Berkshire, SL1-2TB, UK
e-mail: sterlingdis@yahoo.co.uk
New Dawn Press (An Imprint of Sterling Publishers (P) Ltd.)
A-59, Okhla Industrial Area, Phase-II, New Delhi-110020
e-mail: sterlingpublishers@airtelbroadband.in
www.sterlingpublishers.com

Women Administrators: Challenges in the New Millennium
© 2006, Dr. B. Madhana Rekha
ISBN 1 932705 63 5

All rights are reserved.
No part of this publication may be reproduced, stored in a retrieval system or transmitted, in any form or by any means, mechanical, photocopying, recording or otherwise, without prior written permission of the original publisher.

PRINTED IN INDIA

*Dedicated to My Beloved Parents,
Husband, Daughter Amy, Son Andrew and
all members of my family*

Preface

Women's representation in the policy-making process is dismally low despite the fact that they constitute half of the total population of India. While the representation of women and entrance of women into the policy-making process is in itself a great challenge before women administrators, there are far greater issues involved in the journey of women to the top positions. The number of women police officers in the country in top ranks is still very less compared to their male counterparts. People believe that women are not suitable or physically capable of working as members of the police service. This presumption is simply not correct.

Women do think that they could get justice only if more and more women are employed in police services as crimes against women like rapes, murders, domestic violence, sexual abuse, eve teasing, sexual harassment in workplaces, dowry harassment etc. are on the increase and have become a daily occurrence. Hence a study was undertaken to highlight the negligible representation of women administrators in India, the problems they face, the challenges before them in the new millennium, the manner in which they tackle the problems like crimes against women and the various policies formulated for the overall development of women.

In this book, an attempt has been made to discover whether or not women administrators face similar problems compared to other women in the Indian society. The views of women administrators were sought in order to identify whether they consciously work for the upliftment of women. This book has proved that women administrators are living examples of how both the roles of women at home and office could be harmoniously blended. From a situation where women were confined to the traditional occupations like teachers, nurses, and social workers, modern Indian women have entered all walks of life and branched out into non-traditional professions like Indian Administrative Services (IAS) and Indian Police Services (IPS). The apprehension that as women move up the ladder in their jobs, they have to devote increasing time to their work responsibilities thereby jeopardising their family obligations is not true.

This book would be beneficial to academicians like students, teachers and researchers of all disciplines especially in the field of social sciences like public administration, political science, women studies, management, sociology, psychology, economics, and history to understand the potentials, problems, challenges and future prospects of women administrators in India. In addition to that, the book would be useful to policy-makers, governments of both central and states, non-governmental organisations, multinational corporations, public and private sectors, other national and international bodies.

Dr. B . Madhana Rekha

Acknowledgements

Women Administrators: Challenges in the New Millennium is an attempt to study the nature of problems the women executives face, the nature of discriminations they encounter and to compare their status and position with their less fortunate counterparts elsewhere. The attitudes of women administrators in Tamil Nadu on the various contentious socio-economic and political issues are also studied.

I am thankful to all the women administrators in Tamil Nadu who provided their accessibility and spared their valuable time in filling up the questionnaires and expressing their views openly to me.

My special thanks to the University Grants Commission, New Delhi for selecting me as a junior research fellow and providing me the financial support during the study.

My sincere thanks are to my supervisor Prof. and Head, M. Suresh Babu, Department of Public Administration, Madras Christian College, Chennai and my late Prof. R. Stephen Samuel for the encouragement he had given.

Though it is not possible to mention all my friends and well wishers who assisted me at various stages of this work, I remember them with gratitude.

No words can adequately express my debt of gratitude to my mother, late Mrs. D. Deva Krupa Balaraman and my father Mr. V. Balaraman, Regional Director (Rtd.), National Savings Organisation for generating in me a perennial interest in higher studies.

Lastly, I would like to thank my husband, Dr. R. Moses Inbaraj, reader, Department of Zoology, Madras Christian College and my beloved children Amy Moses and Andrew Moses for their constant support and help to publish this book.

Above all I would like to acknowledge God Almighty who enabled me to complete this book.

Contents

Preface		vii
Acknowledgements		ix
	Introduction	1
1.	Socio-economic Background	12
2.	Women Administrators in their Offices	45
3.	Women Administrators at Home	65
4.	Attitudes towards Social Change	79
5.	Opinion about Political System	106
6.	Perspective on Economic Development	123
	Conclusion and Suggestions	134
	Bibliography	144
	Index	159

Introduction

The public administrative system plays a major role in implementing various public policies and programmes formulated by the government for the socio-economic and politico-cultural development of the country.

In modern times, an efficient administrative machinery cannot be conceived without an efficient civil service. Under a parliamentary system of government like India, in theory, ministers decide the policy and the civil servants carry out their decisions. But in reality the ministers have neither the time, nor the knowledge or skill, to formulate policies without the assistance of the civil servants.

A government may be conducted without parliament for some time or even without ministers, but it would be impossible for a society to manage its affairs without a well-organised, efficient and honest civil services. Therefore, civil servants are indispensable in any modern government. Indeed, it will be no exaggeration to give public administration the status of the *fourth* organ of the government.

However, in the new millennium challenges before administrators is enormous because they are working in an unsympathetic and unrewarding political environment. Pressures on administrators are mounting day-by-day. There is a vast increase in the tasks and changes in the nature of roles performed by civil servants. Moreover, the importance of policy-making has been steadily increasing over the years and today civil servants are compelled to work under political directions and they are under the glare of public accountability. The traditional concept of being anonymous has also been challenged of late. Administrators have to canvass support for a government policy and seek people's participation in the execution of a policy. So, administrators are no longer mere executors of minister's orders. They have to initiate, sell, evoke support and enthusiasm of the people to implement any policy. It is not enough if they merely respond to popular demands and needs of people but also have to be accountable for their actions.

Political interference in administration especially from the ruling party is steadily increasing. Even transfer and postings take on a political basis. Transfer is also used as a weapon to compel an official concerned to do or not to do something as desired by a politician. Ministers have a tendency to make the officials the scapegoat for all acts of omission and commission in their charge. There is also a general distrust of civil servants among members of parliament and a feeling that the administration is invariably inefficient. Quite often ministers criticise the civil servants on the floors of legislature. Such an attitude demoralises the civil servants. Public expectations have also gone up and when they are not fulfilled, people also resort to criticism and put pressure on the officials. As the public relations are very weak on the official side, people do not understand the actual difficulties of the administration. These factors affect the morale of the officials and it further deteriorates during political instability. So there is a development of unhealthy trend of politicisation of civil servants. At times they even escape or evade responsibilities. In extreme cases honest and efficient[1] officers have preferred to resign rather than face humiliation.

Bureaucratic Theory

The word 'bureaucracy' lends itself to two usages. It refers to the tasks and procedures of administration. It is also used as a collective noun referring to a body of administrative officials. Frequently it also stands for inefficiency and an improper exercise of power on the part of officials, and thus has become a term of abuse. The word 'bureaucracy' was coined by the French economist Vincent de Gournay (1712-1759).

However, it was Max Weber (1864-1920) who founded the modern sociological study of bureaucracy. Bureaucracy as enunciated by Max Weber is based on the notion of *rational-legal authority*, that is, an authority which employees recognised as legitimate being inherent in the administrators in the hierarchical structure.

Each position in the bureaucracy has its duties and rights which are all clearly defined by rules and procedures which have been laid down to determine how the given authority is to be exercised. Bureaucracy promises a stable organisation, despite the fact that its incumbents come and go. Its functioning does not necessarily depend on the know how of individuals working in it, but it is embodied in rules, regulations, procedures and other written records which always remain within the organisation in contrast to individuals who could join and leave.

The following are the characteristics of bureaucracy, as enumerated by Max Weber:

1. The officials are personally free and subject to authority only with respect to their *impersonal* official obligations.

2. They are organized in a clearly defined *hierarchy* of occupies.

3. Each office has a clearly defined sphere of *competence* in the legal sense.

4. The office is filled by a free *contractual* relationship. Thus in priniciple, there is free selection.

5. Candidates are selected on the basis of *technical qualifications* in a rational manner. They are tested by examination or guaranteed by diplomas certifying technical training, or both. They are appointed and not elected.

6. They are remunerated by *fixed salaries* in money for the most part, with a right to pensions. Only under certain circumstances does the employing authority, especially in private organisations, have a right to terminate the appointment, but the official is always free to resign. The salary scale is primarily graded according to rank in the hierarchy but, in addition to this criterion, the responsibility of the position and the requirements of the incumbent's social status may be taken into account.

7. The office is treated as the sole, or at least the *primary occupation* of the incumbent.
8. It constitutes a career. There is a system of *'promotion'* according to seniority or achievement. Promotion is dependent on the judgement of superiors.
9. The official is *not involved in the ownership* of the means of administration.
10. He is subject to strict and systematic *discipline and control* in the conduct of the office.

Other attributes of bureaucracy are hierarchy, division of labour and functional specialisation. These ten features constituted Max Weber's ideal, pure or rational type of bureaucracy. The Weberian bureaucracy emerged as a neutral hierarchically organised, efficient and a powerful part of contemporary society.

The characteristics of bureaucracy should be precision, continuity, discipline, strictness and reliability. These characteristics make it technically the most efficient form of organization. Max Weber has defined bureaucracy in terms of its structural characteristics. The above mentioned attributes portray a kind of organization which is impersonal where authority is exercised by administrators only by virtue of the office they hold and what is more, in accordance with clearly defined rules and regulations. In other words, bureaucracy emerges as uniquely impersonal, neutral, passive, and instrumental. Its behavioural characteristics are objectivity, precision and consistency.[2] But we should keep in mind that modern bureaucracy is quite different from the ideal one of Max Weber.

Richard H. Hall[3] has tabulated the characteristics of bureaucracy as listed by a number of authors, including Weber, Litwak, Friedrich, Merton, Udy, Heady, Parsons and Berger. From the longer roster of characteristics, Hall picked up six dimensions of bureaucracy for special attention. These are (1) a well defined hierarchy of authority, (2) a division of labour based on functional specialization, (3) a system of rules covering the rights and duties of positional incumbents, (4) a system of procedures for dealing with work situations, (5) impersonality of interpersonal relationships and (6) selection for employment and promotion based on technical competence. This list can serve very well as a summary of the most commonly mentioned structural hallmarks of bureaucracy.

Certain negative behavioural traits have been added which are dysfunctional, pathological, or self defeating and frustrate the attainment of organizational goals. Robert Merton[4] has made the classic statement of this point of view. He is concerned with the fact that "the very elements which conduce towards efficiency in general produce inefficiency in specific instances" and also "lead to an over concern with strict adherence to regulations which induces timidity, conservation and technicality". Michael Crozier[5] in his valuable study, "The Bureaucratic Phenomenon", describes bureaucracy as a scientific attempt to understand better this "malady of bureaucracy". He explains that the subject to which he refers in speaking of the "bureaucratic phenomenon" is that of the mal adaptations, the inadequacies, or, to use Merton's expressions, the *"dysfunctions"* which necessarily develop within human organisations.

The Origin of the Civil Service

The origin of the civil service goes far deep into the past. It originated in the 'water works civilisation' i.e., the valley of the Nile, the Ganges, the Yangtse and the Euphrates. Since this civilisation depended on large-scale water works, either by way of control of inundation or irrigation, they employed large number of men to look after these. Where this civilisation grew up first is a point on which historians differ. To quote Sardar Panicker, "whether such civilization grew up first in the river valley of India, Egypt, Sumeria or China, it was difficult to say, for when our historical vision opened in the middle of the third millennium organised states were seen existing in all those areas". Thus the civil service may be said to be as old as the civilisation itself. As far back as 2000 BC (2200 BC to 1905 BC) the Chinese had organised a civil service, recruitment to which was based on the principles of merit.[6]

The Civil Services in India

When Indian administration came into the light of authentic history it was as a fully organised bureaucracy. The bureaucracy represented the royal authority and enforced the royal will at all times even against the popular will. Loyalty to the kind was the sole test of continuance in office.

Blunt says[7], "The term civil service was used by the East India company as a name for its establishment of non-military or civilian employees in India". According to O'Malley[8], the term civil service was applied to the general body of persons employed on non-combatant work connected with the administration of a state. He said that the credit for streamlining the service, and creating a real civil service goes to Warren Hastings who set the revenue administration in order, purified trade and took measures to check corruption. O'Malley also said that Warren Hastings laid the foundations of a civil service in the modern sense so far as India is concerned.[9] His successor in office Lord Cornwallis too spared no pains to organize the service on a sound foundation and effected all round reforms. Staff in excess were dispensed with and unauthorised gains were stopped. Therefore it could be said that the former laid the foundations on which the latter built up the superstructure.[10]

In 1853 the competitive examination was introduced, but no Indian could enter the Indian Civil Service (ICS) till the services were transferred to the control of the Crown. The monopoly of the members of the ICS for all important civil appointments was maintained by the Indian Civil Service Act 1861.[11]

The ICS was the elite of the services of the Crown in India. When the British left India there were ten All India Services and twenty-two Central Services. The structure of services underwent a change after independence. The number of All India Services was reduced to only two, i.e., the Indian Administrative Service (IAS) and the Indian Police Service (IPS). The Indian Administrative Service replaced the former Indian Civil Service. However, the members of the Indian Civil Service continued to be known by their former designation. Indian Police came to be designated as Indian Police Service as before 1933.[12]

Introduction

At present there are three All India Services along with 15 Group 'A' and 8 Group 'B' Central Services.[13]

- (i) Indian Administrative Service.
- (ii) Indian Foreign Service.
- (iii) Indian Police Service.

Group 'A'

- (iv) Indian P&T Accounts and Finance Service.
- (v) Indian Audit and Accounts Service.
- (vi) Indian Customs and Central Excise Service.
- (vii) Indian Defence Accounts Service.
- (viii) Indian Revenue Service.
- (ix) Indian Ordinance Factories Service (Assistant Manager, Non Technical).
- (x) Indian Postal Service.
- (xi) Indian Civil Accounts Service.
- (xii) Indian Railway Traffic Service
- (xiii) Indian Railway Accounts Service.
- (xiv) Indian Railway Personnel Service.
- (xv) Posts of Assistant Security Officer in Railway Protection Force.
- (xvi) Indian Defence Estates Service.
- (xvii) Indian Information Service (Junior Grade).
- (xviii) Posts of Assistant Commandant in Central Industrial Security Force.

Group 'B'

- (xix) Central Secretariat Service (Section Officers' Grade).

(xx) Railway Board Secretariat Service (Section Officers' Grade).

(xxi) Armed Forces Head Quarters Civil Service (Assistant Civil Staff Officiers' Grade).

(xxii) Customs Appraisers' Service.

(xxiii) Delhi and Andaman & Nicobar Islands Civil Service.

(xxiv) Delhi and Andaman & Nicobar Islands Police Service.

(xxv) Posts of Deputy Superintendent of Police in the Central Bureau of Investigation.

(xxvi) Pondicherry Civil Service.

Women in Civil Service

After independence in 1948 the central government ended the prohibition against women taking Higher Civil Service examinations. However, restrictions remained. Only unmarried women or widows without encumbrances could join the services, and the government reserved the right not to select a woman even if she qualified through the examination process. The first woman administrator Anna Malhotra a Christian from Kerala, joined IAS in 1951, but the selection committee tried to persuade her to join Indian Foreign Service (IFS) as it was doubted whether women could be able to shoulder responsibilities of law and order in the districts.[14]

The IAS (recruitment) rules 1954 debarred the appointment of married women as a matter of right. IAS (recruitment) rules as well as Indian Police Service (recruitment) rules laid down, "..........No married women shall be entitled as a matter of right to be appointed to the service and where a woman appointed to the service subsequently marries, the Central Government may, if the maintenance of efficiency of service so requires call upon her to resign".[15]

When the recruitment rules were being discussed in the Rajya Sabha the above strictures were vehemently criticised on the floor of the house. The women members attacked them as discrimination against sex and alleged that these deprived them of their constitutionality. This was branded as treacherous and an insult to the women of the country. Even some of the male members made identical observations.[16]

The twenty fourth session of the All India Women's Conference held at Phalton, on the 23rd February 1955, passed a resolution recording their protest against this discrimination. The government spokesman took shelter behind the argument that it was only a permissive clause, the rationale of which had been discussed. Further, they also pointed out that a woman in class I service at that time had married and was allowed to continue.[17] This rule was finally deleted in 1972 after women members of parliament (MPs) denounced it in the parliament.[18] Later, around 1956 there were only seven women officers in the IAS and five in IFS. In IPS there were none. However, their entry into service had been favoured by the Union Public Service Commission (U.P.S.C).[19] The number of women in the Civil Service has been increasing, though as compared to men it is marginal. The Indian Police Service acquired its first woman police officer Kiran Bedi (IPS), a Sikh from the Punjab, in 1972. And within a year it had seven women police officers. Indian Administrative Service had 111 women officers in 1972, the figure rose to 218 in 1977. The representation is even less among scheduled caste and scheduled tribes.[20]

The Role of Higher Civil Service in Developmental Activities

The planning of a uniform system of district administration in modern India was first carried out by Warren Hastings (1772-85) who created on 14th May 1772 the Office of the Collector, with revenue and judicial functions united in the same person. Changes from time to time were effected in the Constitution of that office to suit policy requirements. But imperial considerations as well as the heterogenous character of Indian society finally combined to settle down in the post Mutiny period to a form of district administration where the collector united in his/her office on a permanent basis not only for settlement and collection of revenues, but also in the administration of magisterial, and criminal judicial functions. He/she remained the executive head of the district.[21]

District officers provided relief against petty tyrannies which formed part of their duties to look after the promotion of agriculture, to help projects for improvement, to administer relief, to recommend suspension or remission of land revenue in the event of natural calamities, to preserve peace among agricultural classes, and in short, to secure the welfare of the whole community living in the district. These were the functions which remained traditionally attached to the office.[22] By virtue of experience, historical position and status in the superior civil service, the Collector alone as the head of the district administration, could represent in their totality the policy, will and might of the Government. They continued through the ages to function in some form or other despite political instability at the centre or in the provinces. They still continue so even now.

The sub-divisional system grew with the extended function of the state, especially to meet the exigencies of relief operations against famines and epidemics, not only involving in places the problems of law and order on a mass scale, but also dictating the necessity of creating the self-governing institutions of local bodies as agencies to raise local resources for local needs in respect of such development activities as roads, sanitation, education, public health and the like.[23]

The administrative work in a nation such as India can be extremely varied. Female IAS officers start their careers as assistant collectors or sub-divisional magistrates in the districts where they work under more experienced administrators in the law and order and revenue operations. After several years in the districts women are usually assigned to government secretariats in the state or national capital and may travel up the ladder in one ministry or work in several. A mid-level job in the agricultural ministry might involve drafting policies for irrigation projects in a state and evaluating the cost-benefit ratios achieved by the projects. A mid-level job in the Railway Ministry might involve supervising the payroll budget for railway employees and participating in negotiations with the unions. A high-level job in the Social Welfare Ministry might involve framing policies for government, women's programs, encouraging other ministries to develop programs and evaluating all the state level programs for women's welfare.[24]

Introduction 11

Notes and References

[1] Avasthi, Amreshwar & Anand Prakash Avasthi, *Public Administration in India*, ed., Lakshmi Narain Agarwal, 7th Revised Edition, Agra, 2001, pp.365-381.
[2] Maheshwari, S. R., "Bureaucracy or Bureaucratic Theory" *Employment News*, Volume XVII, no. 29 (1992): p.1.
[3] Hall, Richard H. "Intraorganisational Structural Variation: Application of the Bureaucratic Model", *Administrative Science Quarterly* 7, no. 3 (1962): 295-308.
[4] Merton, Robert, "Bureaucratic Structure and Personality in Social Theory and Social Structure", *Free Press of Glencoe Inc.*, New York, 1949, pp. 361-371.
[5] Crozier, Micael, *The Bureaucratic Phenomenon*, Chicago: University of Chicago Press, 1964, pp. 4-5.
[6] Sinha, V.M., "The Superior Civil Services in India – A Study in Administrative Development (1947-1957)", *IRAS*, Jaipur, 1985, p.1.
[7] Blunt, E.A.H., *The Indian Civil Service*, London: Faber and Faber, 1937, p.1.
[8] O'Malley, L.S.S., *The Indian Civil Service: 1601-1930*, London: Frank Cass Cass Co., 1965, p. 1.
[9] Ibid., p. 28.
[10] Ibid., p. 23.
[11] Sinha, Op. cit., p. 12.
[12] Ibid., p. 26-28.
[13] *Employment News* (Special Supplement), 11-17 February 1995, p. 33.
[14] Everett, Jana, "Women in Law and Administration", in Joyce Lebra & Others ed., "*Women and Work: Continuity and Change*", New Delhi: Promilla & Co. Publishers, 1984, p. 241.
[15] Sinha, Op.cit., p. 45.
[16] Ibid., p. 46.
[17] Ibid., p. 47-48.
[18] Sahai, Nisha, "Women in Administration: A Growing Phenomenon", *Directory of Indian Women Today*, ed. Aijiet Cour, New Delhi: India International Publishers, 1976, pp. 25-28.
[19] Sinha, Op.cit., p. 49.
[20] Desai, Neera & Vibhuti Patel, *Indian Women Change & Challenge in the International Decade 1975-85*, Bombay: Popular Prakashan Pvt. Ltd., 1990, p. 35.
[21] Misra, B. B., *Government and Bureaucracy in India: 1947-1976* (Delhi: Oxford University Press, 1986), p. 338.
[22] Misra, B. B., "Evolution of the Office of Collector", *Indian Journal of Public Administration*, July-Sep, 1965.
[23] Misra, Op.cit., pp. 339-340.
[24] Everett, Jana, Op.cit., p. 244.

1
Socio-economic Background

Introduction

An individual's birth in a particular family, region and religious faith not only determines his/her life opportunities but also provides him/her with a specific outlook towards life. The factors which influence lifestyle can be broadly divided into two: ascriptive and achieved. The former includes the familial race, kinship, linguistic groups and religion for example. The latter includes an individual's education, occupational skills, economic, social position, the friendship circle, the types of the house, the locality in which he/she lives amongst many factors. Consequently an individual's lifestyle and his/her personality make-up are the outcome of his/her assigned as well as achieved background factors and his/her own life experiences.[1]

It is often stated that the Indian bureaucracy is dominated by upper middle class entrants who do not perceive the priorities of a system dominated by the agrarian core. Therefore, the bureaucracy is expected to come out of its class character and consequent containing so as to evolve as a genuinely committed services mechanism.[2]

According to Sahai, women in the elite services come from urban upper middle class backgrounds. In this class a high percentage of women have University education. In the last twenty years there has been an increasing acceptance of such women working. Resistance to hiring women in the private sector and parental doubts about the respectability of such careers for their daughters have combined to make government service the preferred occupational choice of upper middle class urban women.[3]

In the recent past, a few studies have been published highlighting the socio-economic background of bureaucrats. Bureaucrats comprise an elite group having sound family status and economic standards, urban upbringing and socialisation, and education at prestigious schools and colleges. Further, a large majority of Indian bureaucrats come from higher castes.[4]

In this book the socio-economic background of women administrators in Tamil Nadu in terms of age, caste, religion, are education, occupation, parental education, income, marital status studied. The findings mainly confirm the result of earlier workings.

Age

The Union Public Service Commission conducts competitive examinations for the recruitment of candidates to the Civil Services. A candidate appearing for the examination must have attained the age of 21 years and should not be above 28 years. However, the upper age limit is relaxable for various categories as follows:

(i) Up to a maximum of five years if a candidate belongs to a scheduled caste or a scheduled tribe.

(ii) Up to a maximum of three years if a candidate is a bona fide repatriate of Indian origin from Kuwait or Iraq and has migrated to India from any of these countries.

(iii) Up to a maximum of eight years if a candidate belongs to a scheduled caste or a scheduled tribe and is also a bonafide repatriate of Indian origin from Kuwait or Iraq and has migrated to India from any of these countries.

(iv) Up to a maximum of three years in the case of defence services personnel, disabled in operations during hostilities with any foreign country or in a disturbed area and released as a consequence thereof.

(v) Up to a maximum of eight years if a candidate belongs to a scheduled castes or a scheduled tribe and is also a defence service personnel, disabled in operations during hostilities with any foreign country or in a disturbed area and released as a consequence thereof.

(vi) Up to a maximum of five years in the case of ex-servicemen including commissioned officers and ECOs/SSCOs who have rendered at least five years of military service and have been released (a) on completion of assignment otherwise than by way of dismissal or discharge on account of misconduct or inefficiency, or (b) on account of a physical disability attributable to military service or (c) on invalidity.

(vii) Up to a maximum of ten years in the case of ex-servicemen including commissioned officers and ECOs/SSCOs who belong to the scheduled castes or scheduled tribes and who have rendered at least five years military service and have been released (a) on completion of assignment otherwise than by way or dismissal or discharge on account of misconduct of inefficiency or (b) on account of physical disability attributable to military service or (c) on invalidity.

(viii) Up to a maximum of five years in the case of ECOs/SSCOs who have completed an initial period of assignment of five years of military service and whose assignment has been extended beyond five years and in whose case the Ministry of Defence issues a certificate that they can apply for civil employment and will be released on three months notice on selection from the data of receipt of offer of the appointment.

(ix) Up to maximum of ten years in the case of candidates belonging to scheduled castes or scheduled tribes who are also ECOs/SSCOs and have completed an initial period of assignment of five years of military service and whose assignment has been extended beyond five years and in whose case the Ministry of Defence issues a certificate that they can apply for civil employment and will be released on three months notice on selection from the date of receipt of offer of appointment.

(x) Up to a maximum of three years in the case of candidates belonging to other backward classes who are eligible to avail reservation applicable to such candidates.

Bhambhri's[5] study showed that 52.5% of the bureaucrats were below 25 years and Chaturvedi's[6] findings revealed that the executive category was largely in the 25-30 years of age bracket. The Table 1.1a below shows that the women administrators were of different age groups. Around 6.25% of the respondents were between 25-30 years, 25% of the respondents were between 30-35 years, 25% of the respondents were between 35-40 years and 25% years were between 40-45 years. About 8.75% of the respondents were between 45-50 years. These findings differed from the findings of Chaturvedi.

Table 1.1a. Age Group of Women Administrators

Age group in years	25-30	30-35	35-40	40-45	45-50	no response	Total
%	6.25	25.00	25.00	25.00	8.75	-	100.00

The Table 1.1b shows the correlation of age vs experience of the administrators. It is clear from the Table that the experience of the administrators increased with their age.

Table 1.1b shows the relationship between the age and income of the respondents. It is clear that 68.75% of the respondents had a monthly income above Rs. 7,000/-. The lowest income of the respondents was Rs. 3,000 to 4,000 and they were in the age group of 30-35 years. It is also interesting to note that the younger respondents got higher income compared to the older respondents. About 6.25% of the respondents in the age group 25-30 years got an income of Rs 4,000 to 5,000, whereas 12.5% of the respondents in the age group of 30-35 years got Rs. 3,000 to 4,000. This could be due to the early entrance to the service by the younger respondents when compared to the older respondents and also due to the prevailing pay structures at that time. 12.5% of the respondents were from Rs. 6,000/- to 7,000/- income group. The majority of the respondents who got a monthly income above Rs. 7,000/- were between 25-40 years of age.

Table 1.1b. Age and Monthly Income of Women Administrators

Monthly Income	Age					
	25-30	30-35	35-40	40-45	45-50	Total
Rs. 3000-4000	-	12.50	-	-	-	12.50
Rs. 4000-5000	6.25	-	-	-	-	6.25
Rs. 5000-6000	-	-	-	-	-	-
Rs. 6000-7000	-	6.25	6.25	-	-	12.50
Above Rs. 7000	6.25	18.75	25.00	18.75	-	68.75
Total%	12.50	37.50	31.25	18.75	-	100.00

Place of Birth

It is assumed that the city, town or village background of the respondents would definitely have its impact on their upbringing which in turn would have influenced the opportunities for choosing their career. Earlier studies revealed that a larger proportion of administrators belong to the urban setting.[7] The present study agrees with the findings of earlier studies. Table 1.2a shows that 62.5% of the respondents originated from the city background and 31.25% of the respondents were of the village origin.

Table 1.2a Women Administrators' Place of Birth

Place :	City	Town	Village	No response	Total
% :	62.50	31.25	-	6.25	100.00

Table 1.2b shows the relationship of the place of birth to choosing a career. Those respondents who were born in a city setup chose their career because of the influence of their parents, friends and due to their self-determination. This could be due to the exposure and opportunity given to females in the cities to choose their career. However, the respondents who were born in town chose their

career either because of the influence of their parents or teachers and not because of self-determination. Hence the city-born respondents were comparatively more self-determined than the town born respondents. This would definitely influence the administrators when making decisions in their job. The city-born could solve any problem on their own without counting upon others for help at critical situations.

Table 1.2b. Place of Birth and Choosing a Career

Place	City	Town	Village	No response	Total
Influence of parents	25.00	25.000	-	-	50.00
Teachers	-	6.25	-	-	6.25
Friends	25.00	-	-	-	25.00
Self-determination	6.25	-	-	6.25	12.50
Others	6.25	-	-	-	6.25
Total%	62.50	31.25	-	6.25	100.00

Place of Residence

Rural-urban background is another significant factor influencing the decision-making power of women. The respondents residing in rural environment may follow the traditional ideals while the urban residents may resist the traditional role.[8] From Table 1.3 it is very clear that 93.75% of the respondents resided in rural areas, while only 6.25% of the respondents resided in urban settings. It is likely that when the urban background administrators are appointed to decide rural issues they may find it difficult in the initial stages and take some time in making decisions.

Table 1.3. Residence of Women Administrators

Place:	Rural	Urban	Total
%	93.75	6.25	100.00

Caste

Caste has been treated as a comprehensive system of social relations. It has been equated with the Hindu society. There are studies also which have found castes among Muslim, Sikhs and Christians in India. However, the way in which caste has become an ideology pervading the entire Hindu society is not found elsewhere. It is a culturally specific and unique system.

The origin of the caste system dates back to the age of the Rig Veda. The *Purusha Sukta*, a part of the Rig Veda, states that the *Brahmanas, Rajanyas (Kshatriyas), Vaishyas* and *Shudras* sprang from the mouth, arms, thighs and feet of the Purusa (God). Later on, these became castes.[9]

The other very important feature of the caste system is its control over woman's labour. Caste not only determines social division of labour but also sexual division of labour. Certain tasks have to be performed by women while certain other tasks are meant for men. In agriculture for instance, women can engage themselves in water-regulation, transplanting, weeding, but not in ploughing. With upward mobility of the group, women are immediately withdrawn from the outside work. Physical mobility is also restricted through caste norms. The significant symbol of the low status of women in society is that the women of lower castes are permitted to work for men of higher status, while there is a very severe punishment for men of lower castes who dare to approach any women of higher groups.[10]

Srinivas defines caste in the following words, "Caste is a hereditary, endogamous, usually localised group having traditional associations with an occupation and a particular position in the local hierarchy of castes. Relations between castes are governed among other things by the concepts of pollution and purity and generally maximum commensality occurs within the caste".[11]

In this study, the caste of the women administrators in Tamil Nadu has been traced out. Caste in Tamil Nadu was divided into Forward Community (FC) or Other Community (OC), Backward Community (BC), Most Backward Community (MBC) and Scheduled Caste (SC) or Scheduled Tribe (ST) as major castes.

Socio - economic Background

There are subcastes in each caste. Forward caste was considered as the top rung of the ladder, followed by the backward castes and most backward castes and the scheduled castes and tribes were the lowest in the community. The scheduled castes and scheduled tribes were treated as untouchables.

Among the forward castes namely, Brahmins, Mudaliars, Vellalas, Gounders and Chettiars women participate in family decision-making on several issues and in the management of family affairs. But control of finance remains with men. Selection of brides and grooms is made jointly by elderly men and women but property transactions and management remain mostly with men. Women's privileges are much less among several socially backward communities like the SC, STs, with the exception of the Thevars. Among the Thevars, women take decisions in several aspects of family affairs. Among the Chakiliars, the Pallars and the Parayars (SCs) men dominate. Respect for the mother is almost universal in Tamil Nadu, but women as wives and daughters are not respected as much. More than one daughter in a family is unwelcome in most communities. Tamil society being universally patrilineal, sons are in greater demand. The increasing cost of marriage of daughters also makes parents nervous over the birth of daughters. Consequently, neglect and cases of female infanticide are common among certain communities.[12]

Table 1.4a shows that 6.25% of the administrators were SCs 6.25% were MBC, 6.25% of them were BC and 75% of the administrators were from OC which was considered as forward castes. There was no representation of STs. It is clear from the analysis that there is a very low representation of lower castes and three fourths of the administrators belong to higher castes. Hence it could be said that Indian bureaucracy is dominated by high castes.

Table 1.4a. Caste of Women Administrators

Caste:	SC	ST	MBC	BC	OC	No response	Total
%:	6.25	-	6.25	6.25	75.00	-	100.00

Abb: SC - Scheduled Caste
ST - Scheduled Tribe

MBC - Most Backward Community
BC - Backward Class
OC - Other Community (includes upper class)

Jana Everett in her study of women in law and administration found that the I.A.S. women tend to come from high caste families with a tradition of educational achievement over many generations.[13]

Taub's study also revealed that among the I.A.S., 15 members were *Brahmins*, 7 were *Kshatriyas* and one was a *Vaisya*. There were no Sudras amongst them.[14]

This finding could be attributed to the fact that the SC population had a lower level of female literacy at 18.5% relative to the rest of the population, at 39%. The tribal women had even lower proportion of literates among them at 14%. The constitutional directives of providing free and compulsory education for all children up to 14 years of age is as yet unfulfilled.[15]

Table 1.4b shows the relationship of caste to the family head. About 37.5% of the respondents belonging to FC had their husbands as the family head and 31.25% of those belonging to MBC, BC and FC had both their husband and themselves as the heads of the family. Among the SC respondents 6.25% of them acted themselves as the head of the family.

Table 1.4b. Caste and Head of Family of Administrators

Head of family	Caste						Total
	SC	ST	MBC	BC	OC	No response	
Self	6.25	-	-	-	6.25	-	12.50
Husband	-	-	-	-	37.50	-	37.50
Parents	-	-	-	-	6.25	-	6.25
In-Laws	-	-	-	-	6.25	-	6.25
Husband & Wife	-	-	6.25	6.25	12.50	6.25	31.75
No response	-	-	-	-	6.25	-	6.25
Total%	6.25	-	6.25	6.25	75.00	6.25	100.00

Article 46 of the Constitution of India provides: "the State shall promote with special care the educational and economic interests of the weaker sections of the people, and in particular, of the SCs and the STs, and shall protect from social injustice and all forms of exploitation".

Article 17 declares: "Untouchability is abolished and its practice in any form is forbidden. The enforcement of any disability arising out of untouchability shall be an offence punishable in accordance with law.[16]

In view of this constitutional obligation, several provisions have been made, such as the reservation of seats for the SCs in the state assemblies, panchayat raj institutions, and parliament. However, only a few of the posts in the administration reserved for the SCs are actually filled. The same is true in regard to completion of education even up to secondary level.

Table 1.4c presents the relationship between caste and traditional customs followed in the respondents families. The custom of females eating after males was never followed by almost all i.e., 93.75% of the individuals. Only 6.25% of the respondents belonging to forward communities sometimes followed the tradition.

The custom of females not standing before the males was again never followed by any of the respondents belonging to different castes.

The traditional Indian custom of having separate apartment for women was never followed by any of the respondents' families. The family custom of restricting the free movement of women outside the family was not followed by 87.5% of the respondents belonging to backward communities and forward communities. However, 6.25% of the respondents belonging to the SC sometimes followed that custom.

Restriction on mingling with others during menstruation was never followed by the respondents of the different castes. Only 6.25% of the respondents of the other community sometimes followed it.

The Indian custom of giving preferential treatment for boys over girls was not followed by 93.75% of the respondents of the various castes. Sometimes 6.25% of the respondents belonging to other community gave the preferential treatment to boys.

The tradition of restricting women in entertaining or receiving friends was ever made in the families of backward and forward communities. However, 6.25% of the respondents belonging to SC had followed the custom.

Table 1.4c. Caste and Traditional Customs: Females Eating after Males

Caste:	SC	ST	MBC		BC	OC response	No Total
Followed always	-	-	-	-	-	-	-
Some times	-	-	-	-	6.25	-	6.25
Never	6.25	-	6.25	6.25	68.75	6.25	93.75
Total%	6.25	-	6.25	6.25	75.00	6.25	100.00

Hence from the above analysis it is clear that almost all the families of the respondents belonging to the different castes did not follow the traditional customs of suppressing the women. In some cases the custom of females eating after males, restrictions during menstruation, preferential treatment of boys over the girls, were followed in some of the families of the administrators belonging to FC. The custom of the free movement of women outside the family and entertaining friends and relatives was followed in some of the SC families.

This change in the traditional Indian customs was mainly because of modernisation and development in the country. Due to the various developmental programmes and welfare policies introduced by the government, educational standards have improved and education in turn has helped the people to modernise their thinking and to behave in a sophisticated manner. All the age old customs are not followed and people have started thinking in terms of destiny.

Girls in large numbers joined schools and colleges. For the first time they glimpsed a world which was earlier the exclusive domain of men. Women entered the portals of medicine, engineering, the administrative services, politics, law, teaching and the mushrooming business organisations and manufacturing industries. Slowly but steadily they succeeded in joining, what were considered elite professions.[17]

Religion

Religion may be defined as beliefs and practices related to supernatural entities, spirits and powers, which are considered as ultimate in shaping human relations.[18]

India, as a secular nation, accommodates several religions such as Buddhism, Jainism, and Sikhism along with Hinduism, Christianity, Islam and others. The land of India is covered with numerous temples, churches, mosques and gurudwaras. Culturally, Tamil Nadu has a rich variety of famous festivals, functions and feasts. Most of the great temples spread all over the state celebrate several complex festivals in which both men and women participate. In such festivals along with gods, goddesses are worshipped which testifies to the importance given to women in social life. These festivals are accompanied by performances of fine arts such as music, dance, drama, and other traditional varieties of entertainment like instrumental music, (villupattu) acrobatics, games, sports and display of physical strength of animals (cock fights, bull fights). In a non-formal way these centres disseminate and perpetuate the rich cultural tradition of Tamil Nadu.

The princes of the past during the famous dynasties of Cheras, Cholas and Pandyas kingdoms of Tamil Nadu built several architecturally famous and massive temples. Centres of cultural activity also grew and flourished. In the sculptures that adorn the towers and walls of temples, female figures received prominence. This indicates the importance given to women in the remote past.[19]

Religion plays a vital role in one's life. In fact, religion moulds the character and builds up the personality. Hinduism is the predominant religion in India. It has changed due to the spread of scientific knowledge, technological advancement, improved means of communication and the process of secularism. However, Hinduism remains a complex phenomenon, despite changes due to these factors. At the local level, religious practices remain unaffected to a large extent.

Table 1.5a shows the religion of women administrators in Tamil Nadu. 75% of the respondents were Hindus. Only 12.5% were muslims and 12.5% were Christians. Other religions were not found in the administrative service.

Table 1.5a. Religion of Women Administrators

Religion:	Hindu	Muslim	Christian	Other	Total
%:	75.00	12.50	12.50	-	100.00

There is a possibility of respondents being inclined towards the issues of Hindus rather than other religions. They might look into the needs and problems of Hindus immediately when compared with other religions.

Table 1.5b compares religion with family type. Only respondents belonging to Hindu and Muslim religions in some cases were living in joint families. None of the Christians lived in joint families. However, the majority of the respondents, irrespective of their religion were living as nuclear families. This could be because of their place and nature of work. Even though the majority of the respondents were Hindus, they did not live in joint families. This pattern of living has been brought about by modernisation, urbanisation and socio-economic change.

Table 1.5b Religion and Family Type of Women Administrators

Religion:	Hindu	Muslim	Christian	Other	Total
Nuclear family	68.75	6.25	12.50	-	87.50
Joint family	6.25	6.25	-	-	12.50
Total %	75.00	12.50	12.50	-	100.00

Table 1.5c shows religion and family customs. The custom of females eating after males was found sometimes in the joint families of those who were Hindus. This custom was never followed by any other religion. The Hindu tradition of respecting males by serving food first and then to females was followed. Even when there was not sufficient food for females they tended to manage with what was left over.

The custom of females not standing in the presence of males and separate apartments for women were never followed by any of the religions represented amongst the respondents. This is because women settled away from the partrilocal village and in urban areas and so had greater freedom of association and movement, particularly if they also contributed to the family economy.[20]

Table 1.5c. Religion and Traditional Customs: Females Eating after Males

Religion:	Hindu	Muslim	Christian	Other	Total
Followed always	-	-	-	-	-
Some times	6.25	-	-	-	12.50
Never	68.75	12.50	12.50	-	93.75
Total%	75.00	12.50	12.50	-	100.00

The customs like restriction on the freedom of movement of women outside the family, and mingling with others during menstruation, giving preferential treatment to boys over girls, and restriction of women entertaining or receiving friends was sometimes followed in joint families of the Hindu respondents. The Hindu culture puts tremendous weight on the minds of Indians. In addition to that, the existence of the religion from times unknown has its effect on the people. Therefore it is clear that some of the declarations and practices of Hinduism could account for the lowering of the status of women.

Language

"A language is a system of arbitrary vocal symbols by which members of a social group co-operate and interact". (*Gazetteer of*

India, Vol.I). Language as a system, consists of a series of symbols, the meanings of which must be learnt by all those who use that language. Language is an aspect of culture "by means of which the learning process is effectuated and a given way of life achieves both continuity and change". (*Gazetteer of India*, Vol.I). The building-up of knowledge is not possible without language.

The Constitution of India, in its eighth schedule, recognised 15 languages. These are Assamese, Bengali, Gujarati, Hindi, Kannada, Kashmir, Malayalam, Marathi, Oriya, Punjabi, Sanskrit, Sindhi, Tamil, Telugu and Urdu. Hindi has been given the status of India's official language along with English.[21]

The Tamil language spoken in Tamil Nadu is the second most ancient language of India, next to Sanskrit and formed the root of most of the other Dravidian languages i.e., Kannada, Malayalam and Telugu spoken in the southern India. A major classical work of Tamil literature, Tirukura, is a treasure house of knowledge, philosophy, culture and the history of Tamil tradition itself.[22]

Table 1.6a shows the mother tongue of the respondents. Only 31.25% of the respondents' mother tongue was Tamil and 68.75% of the respondents' mother tongue was other languages such and Marathi, Kashmiri, Hindi, Urdu, Telugu and Malayalam. This is because in All India Services to promote national integration, the candidates are given the option to answer all the question papers except the language papers in any one of the Indian languages included in the Eighth Schedule to the Constitution or in English. No more than 50% of those recruited from a given state can be assigned to the state. Most of those who are recruited to the I.A.S prefer to serve in their own state, only those who score highest in the competitive exams have their choice of services and of state cadres provided there is a vacancy in that State. Members of the All India Services are considered to be 'Generalists' who are able to handle a variety of diverse substructive areas.[23]

Table 1.6a. Mother Tongue of Women Administrators

Mother Tongue	Tamil	Other than Tamil	Total
% :	31.25	68.75	100.00

Hence the administrative system consists of varied language speaking officers. Table 1.6b shows the medium of instruction of administrators at school. 25% of the respondents had their local language as their medium of instruction. About 18.75% of them had English and 56.25% of them had languages other than Tamil as their medium of instruction at school. This shows that the candidates appearing for UPSC exams need not necessarily have English as their medium of instruction.

Table 1.6b. Medium of Instruction in School

School medium	Total%
Local language (Tamil)	25.00
English	18.70
Other languages	56.25
Total	100.00

Table 1.6c presents the medium of instruction of women administrators at college. 100% of the respondents had English as their medium of instruction at college. This is because the candidates presenting for the Civil Service Examinations must compulsorily qualify in English which is equivalent to matriculation standard.

Table 1.6c. Medium of Instruction in College

College medium	Total%
Local language (Tamil)	-
English	100.00
Other languages	-
Total	100.00

Table 1.6d presents the type of magazines the respondents read. About 43.75% of the respondents read national magazines and 56.25% of them read both local and national magazines.

Table 1.6d. Types of Magazines the Women Administrator Read

Magazines	Total %
Local	-
National	43.75
Local and National	56.25
Total	100.00

Similarly Table 1.6e highlights the different types of newspapers the respondents read. 37.5% of them read national newspapers and 62.5% of them read both local and national newspapers. The administrators are required to know the state language in which they are posted in order to move cordially with the state Government officials, politicians and the public.

Table 1.6e. Daily Newspapers the Respondents Read

Newspapers	Total%
Local	-
National	37.50
Local and National	62.25
Total	100.00

Posts of the Respondents

The higher administrative posts are staffed by members of the All India Services (Indian Administrative Service - I.A.S, Indian Police Service - I.P.S.). In the All India Services, each officer is assigned a state cadre. The Union Public Service Commission administers competitive examinations for the All India Services. These examinations consist of the written test on nine subjects and an oral interview. The examinations are highly competitive. Candidates have the option to answer all the question papers, except the language papers, viz. Paper I and II in any one of the languages included in the Eighth Schedule to the Constitution or in English.

New recruits to the services are trained at the National Academy of Administration in Mussoorie and at other postings. Members of the All India Services are often 'loaned' to the central government but they remain in the cadre of a particular state. In Indian Civil Service an individual works both in the district and in the state capital or Delhi and in a number of different ministries. Most other services are attached to particular ministries, for example, IPS is attached to the Home Ministry but a regular rotation of assignments is still followed.[24]

In the, Table 1.7a below, it is shown that 81.25% of the respondents were in the IAS posts and only 18.75% of the respondents were holding IPS posts.

Table 1.7a. Posts of Women Administrators

Posts	IAS	IPS	Total
% of respondents	81.25	18.75	100.00

Table 1.7b depicts the posts of the respondents and the occupation of the respondents' husbands. It is interesting to know that 50% of the respondents' husbands were administrators. About 12.5% of them were professionals and 18.75% of them in other jobs. The women administrators chose partners of equal grade. This would help them to have a happy family and better understanding. It is common among women IAS officers to marry their male counterparts whom they meet during the training. Most of the IAS women were married to men in the IAS or other elite services at the same station.[25]

Table 1.7b. Posts of Women Administrators and Occupation of their Husbands

Husband's Occupation	IAS	IPS	Total%
Administration	37.50	12.50	50.00
Professionals	12.50	-	12.50
Others	12.50	6.25	18.75
No response	18.75	-	18.75
Total	81.25	18.75	100.00

Table 1.7c shows the respondents posts with their mother's occupation. It is clear from the Table that 75% of the respondents' mothers were non-working women and only 18.75% of them were in government services. About 6.25% of them were in non-government service and they were not professional women at all.

Table 1.7c. Posts of Women Administrators and occupation of their mothers

Mother's Occupation	IAS	IPS	Total%
Govt Service	18.75	-	18.75
Non-Govt Service	6.25	-	6.25
Professionals	-	-	-
Non-working	56.25	18.75	75.00
Total	81.25	18.75	100.00

Table 1.7d presents the respondents' posts with their father's occupation. It shows that 25% of the respondent's fathers were administrators and 56.25% of them were in government services, and 12.5% of them were professionals. Only 6.25% of them were in non-government services. However, there were none of them who were not working.

Table 1.7d. Posts of Women Administrators and Their Fathers' Occupation

Fathers' Occupation	IAS	IPS	Total%
Govt Service	43.75	12.50	56.25
Non-Govt Service	-	6.25	6.25
Professionals	12.50	-	12.50
Non-working	-	-	-
Administrators	25.00	-	25.00
Total	81.25	18.75	100.00

From the above analysis it is clear that even though majority of the respondents' mothers were non-working their fathers were either administrators and serving in elite or government services. Therefore, the influence of fathers in the choice of public services would have been enormous and they may have inspired their children to take up similar posts.

Socio - economic Background

Work Experience

Table 1.8 shows the work experience of women administrators. The minimum years of experience was found to be 5 and the maximum years of experience was 25 and above. 6.25% of the respondents had work experience up to 5 years. 25% of them had work experience of 5-10 years. 18.75% of them had between 10-15 years. 25.00% of the respondents had 15-20 years of experience, 18.75% of them had between 20-25 years, while 6.25% of the respondents had experience above 25 years. Therefore, it could be said that there were not many new recruits for the past five years in Tamil Nadu.

Table 1.8. Experience of Women Administrators

Years	Up to 5	5-10	10-15	15-20	20-25	25-30	Total
%:	6.25	25.00	18.75	25.00	18.75	6.25	100.00

Monthly Income of the Respondents

Table 1.9 shows the comparison between the respondents' monthly income with their husbands. Majority of the respondents' husbands also got above Rs. 7000/- as their monthly income. Hence it could be said that the financial status of their husbands was almost same when compared with the respondents.

Table 1.9. Income of Women Administrators and Their Husbands' Income

Husbands' Income	Women adminisitrators' Income						Total
	(a)	(b)	(c)	(d)	(e)	(f)	
(a) Rs. 3000-4000/-	-	6.25	-	-	-	-	6.25
(b) Rs. 4000-5000/-	-	-	6.25	-	-	-	6.25
(c) Rs. 5000-6000/-	-	-	-	-	-	-	-
(d) Rs. 6000-7000/-	-	-	-	-	-	6.25	6.25
(e) above Rs.7000	-	-	-	-	12.50	43.75	56.25
(f) no response	-	6.25	-	-	-	18.75	25.00
Total	-	12.50	6.25	-	12.50	68.75	100.00

Type of Family

No society can exist without having institutions of kinship, marriage and family. It is the family which puts together husband and wife, children and other kin under the same roof.

Family in India has remained a vital institution and a foremost primary group because it is the sheet anchor of the patriarchal authority on the one hand and a protector and defender of individual members' (including women) right to property on the other. Despite several wide ranging changes in Indian society because of the synthesis between collectivism and individualism, the Hindu family continues to be joint, partly structurally and mainly functionally and it has not disintegrated into individual families as in Western countries. Several studies on family have revealed that industrialisation, urbanisation, education and migration have not necessarily resulted into nuclearisation of family in India. Even the nuclear family in India is not simply a conjugal family. A real change in the family must refer to the changed pattern of kinship relations, obligations of members towards each other, and individualisation. In other words not only change in the composition or structure of family but also its functions must change.[26] According to Irawati Krave, "A joint family is a group of people who generally live under one roof, who eat food cooked in one kitchen, who hold property in common, participate in common family worship and are related to one another as some particular type of kindred."[27]

Table 1.10a. Type of Family of Women Administrators

Family	Nuclear family	Joint family	Total
%	87.50	12.50	100.00

Table 1.10a shows the type of family of women administrators. About 87.5% of the respondents' families were the nuclear type and only 12.5% of them were joint family type. From the Table it is clear that modernisation has not weakened the joint family system. Even among the educated families the influence of the Hindu culture of observing a joint family system did not break.

Table 1.10b. Family Type and Caste

Caste	Nuclear family	Joint family	Total
SC	6.25	-	6.25
ST	-	-	-
MBC	6.25	-	6.25
BC	6.25	-	6.25
OC	68.75	6.25	75.00
No response	-	6.25	6.25
Total	87.50	12.50	100.00

It is clear from Table 1.10b that higher education does not weaken joint family system, and since higher education is found more among the upper and upper middle castes, the joint family is more prevalent among them than the lower caste people. In functional terms, joint family is nothing but a structure of obligation among the closest kinsmen.[28] According to the Table 1.10c it is clear that in nuclear family type the respondent themselves or their husbands or both of them acted as the head of the family and in some of the joint families, in-laws still acted as the head of family.

Table 1.10c. Family Type and Head of Family

Family Head	Nuclear family	Joint family	Total
Self	12.50	-	12.50
Husband	37.50	-	37.50
Parents	6.25	-	6.25
In-laws	-	6.25	6.25
Husband & Wife	25.00	6.25	6.25
No response	6.25	-	6.25
Total	87.50	12.50	100.00

Marital Status

Table 1.11a. Marital Status of Women Administrators

	Single	Married	Widow	Divorcees	Total
%	6.25	81.25	-	12.50	100.00

Table 1.11a shows the marital status of the women administrators in Tamil Nadu. Only 6.25% of the respondents were single and 12.5% were divorcees. Majority of the administrators i.e., 81.25% were married and there were no widowed administrators.

Table 1.11b highlights the marital status and the type of marriage. It is clear from the Table that 56.25% of the marriages were love marriages and 37.5% of them were arranged. Of which 12.50% were divorcees. There were no divorcees among respondents who had love marriages. Therefore, it could be said that there is a possibility of arranged marriages ending in divorce because only in arranged marriages, does the girl accept the man because of the elders or parents' choice and compulsion. Promilla Kapur's study also showed that working women try to make a satisfactory adjustment in their married life.[29]

Table 1.11b. Marital Status and Type of Marriage

Marriage	Single	Married	Divorcees	Total%
Love	-	56.25	-	56.25
Arranged	-	25.00	12.50	37.50
No response	6.25	-	-	6.25
Total	6.25	-	-	6.25

Head of Family

The majority of the Indian population follows the patrilineal mode of descent. The male is the perpetuator of the line of the family name. Only the son can perform certain religious duties for the family. Discrimination between the sexes in nutrition, medical care and education is directly related to this attitude. Men are the possessors and inheritors of land and its resources.

In a matrilineal system the lineage is counted through the women but power rests with men in the woman's family. Matrilineal communities are concentrated in the south-western region of the country, among the Nairs, Thiyars and Moplahs (Muslims) of Kerala in Lakshadweep, and in the North-eastern region among the Khasis and Garos of Meghalaya and Assam. Matriliny is associated with an economic system in which women are not dependent on men except among the landed Nairs, though they enjoy full property rights. The Nairs impose many restrictions on women, but Garo, Khasi and women in Lakshadweep enjoy greater freedom of movement because of the contribution that they make to the economy.[30]

The joint family was fundamentally patriarchal during the Vedic period. The male head of the family had absolute control over the family property and partition of property was unknown. Discipline in the family and respect for the elders made property free from claims and contributed to the unity and permanence of the family.

In the later period, there were some changes in the family life. Educated girls wanted to start independent homes. Moreover, employment opportunities were found away from the home town and therefore the nuclear family system came into being. The sons moved out with their own small families. In India whether there is a joint family or a nuclear family, the relationship is very closely knit together.[31]

Table 1.12. Head of Family

Head	%
Self	12.50
Husband	37.50
Parents	6.25
In-laws	6.25
Both (Husband & Wife)	31.25
No response	6.25
Total	100.00

Table 1.12 analyses that who plays the role of the head of family among the families of the respondents. Nearly 12.5% of the respondents themselves acted as the head. About 37.5% of the husbands governed the family. 6.25% of the respondents' parents acted as the head of the family and 6.25% of the respondents' in-laws controlled the family. Around 31.25% of the respondents joined with their husbands and acted as head of family. It is clear from the above Table that the patrilineal system still exists in the modern society where the husbands act as head of family and the joint family characteristic of in-laws acting as head of family is prevalent. However, the nuclear family system where both the partners act as head of family existed and in exceptional cases like that of single women parents or the divorcees, the respondents acted as head of family without any option.

Type of Marriage

Marriage is more than simply a legalised sexual union between a man and woman, it is socially acknowledged and approved. In India, people generally believe that marriage is not between two individuals but it is between two families in terms of bonds it creates between them. Certainly marriage provides recognition of legitimacy to children; it confers acknowledged social status on the offsprings and this is important in terms of inheritance and succession.[32] Education and liberalisation of ideas in urban areas have led to certain changes in patterns of selection of the marriage partner. Some recent surveys conducted have however, revealed a greater preference for arranged marriages among the younger generation. In the pre-independence period young people preferred self choice of partners.[33]

Arranged marriages have many features which highlight the unequal status of a woman. She has to present herself before marriageable boys and their relatives for acceptance. In cities and to some extent in villages too, the girls are subjected to a humiliating parade. In some progressive families such meeting between the boy and the girl and their families is arranged on equal footing. But in majority of families in the middle-class, it is a painful experience for the girls. When the nationalism was at its height during the freedom movement, inter-caste and inter-religious marriages became common.[34]

According to the findings done 56.25% of the women respondents had love marriage and 37.25% had arranged. So it is clear that, love marriages outnumbered the arranged ones because it was common for women administrators to marry male officers in their batch whom they meet during training.

Academic Qualifications of the Respondents

Table 1.13a shows the academic qualification of the respondents. Since graduation is the minimum qualification to enter All India Services, about 6.25% of the respondents were graduates, majority of the administrators i.e., 81.25% of the respondents were post-graduates, and nearly 6.25% were Ph.D's and 6.25% of them were professionals like doctors, engineers and lawyers. Respondents with higher qualification might have made few attempts before the selection into the services or they might have under the prescribed age taken the competitive examinations at the time of graduation.

Table 1.13a. Academic Qualifications of Women Administrators

Qualification	%
Graduate	6.25
Post-Graduate	81.25
Ph.D	6.25
Professional	6.25
Total	100.00

Taub in his study while exploring the education status of the IAS officers said that the large number of officers with advanced degrees did not indicate any love for higher education. Rather, it is in part a product of the recruitment procedure. The minimum age at which one is permitted to take the competitive examination is 21. Since many college students in India graduate when they are 19 or 20, they like to work somewhere until they become eligible to take the examination[35]. Table 1.13b compares the qualification of the respondents with their husbands' qualification. It shows that majority of the respondents (81.25%) were post-graduates while only 25% of the husbands were post-graduates and 37.5% were professionals.

Table 1.13b. Women Administrators' and Their Husbands' Qualifications

Husband Qln.	Women Administrators' Qualification				
	Grad.	PG	Ph. D	Prof.	Total%
Graduate	6.25	6.25	-	-	12.50
PG	-	25.00	-	-	25.00
Ph.D	-	-	6.25	-	6.25
Professional	-	31.25	-	6.25	37.50
No response	-	18.75	-	-	18.75
Total	6.25	81.25	6.25	6.25	100.00

It could be said that the women administrators prefer professional partners and choose those who are either higher or equal to them in qualification. Geeta Chaturvedi in her study reveals that in the executive category, both husbands and wives are almost equally qualified though in technical training women respondents lag behind their husbands. Relatively speaking more wives had postgraduate education.[36]

In the Table 1.13c qualification of the respondents and their mother's qualification is presented. Since 43.75% of the respondents' mothers were qualified up to matriculation standard and very few of them, about 25% were graduates and 12.5% were postgraduates, they would have at least encouraged their daughters to pursue higher education. This could also have been the reason for most of the women administrators being post-graduates. Jana Everetts' findings reveal that two women growing up in modest circumstances had mothers who stressed that they could gain social mobility through education.[37]

Table 1.13c. Women Administrators' Qualifications and Their Mothers' Qualifications

Mother Qln.	Administrators' Qualification				
	Grad.	PG	Ph.D	Prof	Total
Matriculation	-	43.75	-	-	43.75
Graduate	6.25	25.00	6.25	-	37.50
PG	-	12.50	-	6.25	18.75
Researcher	-	-	-	-	-
Professional	-	31.25	6.25	-	37.50
Total	6.25	81.25	6.25	6.25	100.00

According to the Table 1.13d the respondents' qualification is correlated to their fathers' qualification. It is clear that most of the respondents' father were either postgraduates or professionals. Only 12.5% of the fathers were graduates and 6.25% were matriculates. Hence the influence of the fathers on their daughters would have been to a very great extent for the respondents to become administrators.

Table 1.13d. Women Administrators' Qualifications and their Fathers' Qualifications

Fathers' Qln.	Administrators' Qualification				
	Grad.	PG	Ph.D	Prof	Total
Matriculation	-	6.25	-	-	6.25
Graduate	6.25	6.25	-	-	12.50
PG	-	37.50	-	6.25	43.75
Researcher	-	-	-	-	-
Professional	-	31.25	6.25	-	37.50
Total	6.25	81.25	6.25	6.25	100.00

The findings of Jana Everett also reveal that almost all of the IAS women interviewed had mothers and fathers with dissimilar educational background. Their fathers had university education and government or professional career. Most of their mothers had not gone to college and were housewives. However, all the administrators reported that their parents had encouraged both the boys and the girls in their family to excel in schooling.[38]

Place of College Studies

It is generally assumed that the administrators had their education in urban areas because most of the colleges situated in urban areas alone have several optional subjects of study which are useful for the preparation of competitive examinations. According to the findings 81.25% of the respondents had their college education in urban areas and only 12.5% got their degrees from rural areas. Therefore, it is to be realised that several courses should be introduced in the colleges in rural areas in order to encourage people to study further. They could stay in the home town without costing much to the families.

Medium of Instruction

Since English is a compulsory subject to qualify in the Union Public Service Examination, it is believed that civil servants would have had English as their medium of instruction in college. It was found that all the respondents had English as their medium of instruction in college.

Choosing of a Career

It is believed that the influence of the educated parents and those who are well placed in their profession will tend to influence their children in choosing their career and guide them in preparation for the civil service examinations. Table 1.14 shows that 50% of the respondents were influenced by their parents in choosing the career. About 6.25% were influenced by the teachers and 6.25% by their friends. 25% of the respondents chose the career on their own and 12.50% were helped by others in this. Therefore it is clear that parents have a major role in influencing their children.

Table 1.14. Choosing of a Career

Influence of	%
Parents	50.00
Teachers	6.25
Friends	6.25
Self-determination	25.00
Others	12.50
Total	100.00

Career Importance

It is assumed that women administrators who hold high and prestigious posts should consider their career as very important. Since all the policies and programmes become effective only with the effective implementation by the civil servants, their careers should never be taken very lightly. It is upon their decisions that the entire nation rests. Table 1.15 elucidates that 6.25% of the respondents gave importance to their careers and 12.5% to their partners'. Among the respondents, 50% of them considered both husbands' and wives' career as important. 25% of them felt neither of their career to be important. It is clear from the above analysis that in some cases the respondents' career was not given importance. Their position was considered secondary when compared with their partners. This attitude should be changed because both the sexes should be treated equally even in practice and not just in theory.

Table 1.15. Career Importance in Administrators' Family

Career importance	%
Self:	6.25
Husband:	12.50
Husband & Wife:	50.00
Does not apply:	25.00
No responses:	6.25
Total	100.00

Conclusion

Thus from the above analysis the socio-economic background of the women administrators in Tamil Nadu was identified. It was found that the age group of respondents was between 25 to 50 years. The minimum years of experience of the women administrators was 5 and the maximum years of experience was above 25 years. All of them had joined the services between 20 to 25 years of age. It was interesting to find that younger civil servants got higher salaries compared with their older counterparts. This could be because of the early entrance of the young respondents in to the service and also due to the higher pay scales. The majority of the respondents received Rs 7000/- and above as their monthly income.

Most of the respondents were born in city and majority of them resided in an urban setting.

Three fourths of the women administrators were from forward communities and were found to be Hindus. However, majority of the respondents' mother tongue was other than Tamil. There were more women IAS officers than IPS.

Most of the respondents were living as nuclear families and among those who where married many of them had love marriages. They joined along with their husbands and acted as the head of the family.

The majority of the administrators were postgraduates and they received their education from urban areas. The medium of instruction of all the respondents was English.

Most of the respondents' husbands were postgraduates or professionals and half of them were administrators. Even the husbands got Rs. 7000/- and above as their monthly income. Majority of the respondents' mothers' qualification was matriculation or at the most postgraduation. Fathers were mostly postgraduates and even professionals. Most of the respondents' mothers were housewives. However, some of the fathers were administrators and many of them were in government services. They would have definitely been instrumental in choosing the career of their daughters. Among the respondents, most of them considered either theirs or both theirs and their husbands' career

Socio - economic Background 43

as important, while some of them felt that their husbands' career was most important.

Notes and References

[1] Krisonswasdi, Napasri, *Women Executives – A Sociological Study in Role Effectiveness*, Jaipur: Rawat Publications, 1989, p. 35.
[2] Subramanium, V., *Social Background of India's Administrators'*, New Delhi Publication Division, Ministry of Broad Casting, 1971, p. 5.
[3] Sahai, Nisha, 'Women in Administration: A Growing Phenomenon', *Directory of Indian Women Today*, ed. Ajiet Cour, New Delhi, 1976, p.27.
[4] Chaturvedi, Geetha, *Women Administrators of India*, Jaipur: RBSA Publishers, 1985, p. 16.
[5] Bhambhri, C.P., *Administrators in a Changing Society*, New Delhi: National, 1972, p. 110.
[6] Chaturvedi, Op. Cit., p. 17.
[7] Ibid, p. 18
[8] Lalitha Devi, V., *Status and Employment of Women in India*, Delhi: B.R. Publishing Corporation, 1982.
[9] Sharma, K.L., *Indian Society*, New Delhi: NCERT, 1990, pp.87-99.
[10] Desai, Neera and Maithreyi Krishnaraj, *Women and Society in India*, Delhi: Ajantha Publications, 1987, p. 33.
[11] Srinivas, M.N., *Caste in Modern India and Other Essays*, Bombay: Media Promotors and Publishers Pvt. Ltd, 1978, p.3.
[12] Mahadevan, K., *Women and Population Dynamics - Perspectives from Asian Countries*, New Delhi: Saga Publications, 1989, pp. 322-323.
[13] Everett, Jana, "Women in Law and Administration", ed. Jana Everett, Joyce Lebra & Joy Paulson, in *Women and Work: Continuity and Charge*, New Delhi: Promilla & Co. Publishers, 1984, p. 243.
[14] Taub, Richard P., *Bureaucrats under Stress - Administrators and Administration in an Indian State*, Firma K.L.Mukhopadhyay, Calcutta, 1969, p. 63.
[15] *Women in Tamil Nadu - A Profile (Dew)*, The Tamil Nadu Corporation for Development of Women Ltd., Madras, 1986, p. 9
[16] Sharma, Op. cit., p. 104
[17] Parikh, Indira J., and Pulin K. Garg, *Indian Women - An Inner Dialogue*, New Delhi: Sage Publications 1989, pp. 74-97.
[18] Sharma, Op. cit, p. 6.
[19] Mahadeven, Op. cit., p. 321.
[20] Report of the National Committee on the Status of Women (1971-74), ICSSR, New Delhi, 1988, p.20.
[21] Sharma, Op. cit., pp.9-10
[22] Mahadevan, Op.cit., p. 320.
[23] Everett, Op. cit., 1984, p. 240.
[24] Ibid, pp. 239-242.
[25] Sahai, Op. cit., p. 26.
[26] Sharma, Op. cit., pp. 81-84.
[27] Karve, Iravati, *Kinship Organisation in India*, 3rd ed., Bombay: Asia Publishing House, 1968, p. 8.
[28] Sharma, Op. cit., p. 84.

[29] Kapur, Promilla, *Marriage and the Working Women in India*, New Delhi: Vikas Publishing House, 1972, p.77.
[30] Report of the National Committee, Op.cit., pp. 18-19.
[31] Devasundaram Suguna, *Roots of Suppression of Women in India*, CSI Womens Fellowship, Bangalore, 1992, pp. 48-49.
[32] Sharma, Op.cit., p. 78.
[33] Report of the National Committee, Op. cit., p. 21.
[34] Desai, Neera and Maithreyi Krishnaraji, Op. cit., p. 20.
[35] Taub, Op. cit., p. 72.
[36] Chaturvedi, Op. cit., pp. 34-35.
[37] Everett, Op. cit., p. 243.
[38] Ibid, p. 243.

2

Women Administrators in their Offices

Introduction

Women in India have always been found working outside their homes. In the village women have always worked in the fields with their men-folk, for a living. In the urban areas lower class women have been found to be working in factories or on construction sites. But recently educated women from the middle and upper class society also have started taking up jobs so that they can come out of the four walls of their houses.

In the earlier days, when due to various socio-economic and politico-legal reasons middle-class women started taking up jobs, they were supposed to do only those jobs which were considered 'respectable' for them by the society. These jobs, occupations or professions were that of a teacher and later that of a doctor. Working in the offices side by side with men, especially as clerks was considered to be the most 'disrespectable', and women who took up such jobs were looked down upon and were discouraged to do so. However, women in the early Vedic times were also found to be good administrators and many times they went to war. Girls in the ruling families used to receive some military and administrative training. Queens like Nayanika of the Satavahana dynasty (2nd century BC), Prabhavati Gupta of the Vakataka family (4th century AD), Vijayabhattarika of the Chalukya house (7th century AD) and Sugandha and Didda of Kashmir (10th century AD) were found to have successfully administered their kingdoms during the minority of their sons. Rajput princesses have been experts in the use of the armies and direct the government in the hour of need. Kumaradeve, the queen of King Samarasi took over the administration of her Kingdom on her husband's death and repulsed the attacks of kutub-ud-din. Javahir Devi, the queen of King Sanga died fighting at the head of her army while defending Chittor after her husband's death.

In the medieval India, one does not hear much of the activities of women. It was because of the Muslim invasion that they had to be kept under purdah and had to rely on the security offered in their homes and to content themselves to domestic duties. During the British rule an economic situation arose in India, when it became essential for the women of the lower income group to work. The Industrial Revolution in Europe forced the women of Europe to leave their homes for work in factories, in large numbers. The condition of Europe affected India also. The cost of living was increased and so here also women thought of working for a better living. Thus slowly in India, women started entering every type of occupational field.[1]

The Indian bureaucracy faced a difficult transition at independence from the night watchman orientation of the "men who ruled India" to the developmental orientation of administrators in a nation ruled by elected leaders. One aspect of the transition was the gradual integration of women into the administrative hierarchy.[2]

In the IAS, the number of women recruited each year increased by one's and two's in the 1950s, by tens in the 1960s, and by twenties in the 1970s. In 1974, 200 women were in IAS comprising 8.8% of the service.[3] Recently women have obtained the highest scores in the competitive examinations every year. However, there are few women in the specialist services, and as of 1978 Kiran Bedi is still the only woman in the IPS.[4] The recorded Indian history, testifies that policing remained a vestige of male sanctity. At present there are several women IPS officers allocated to different state police. The centre maintains its own cadre of IPS and allocates IPS officers to the states. There is a separate pay scale for them as compared to the State cadre. The union government controls the top management and provides a coordinating system of administration for the Indian Police.[5]

Women Administrators at Work

Offices are places of work where women perform beyond their traditional roles. By doing in white collar jobs women assume the male role and activities. Women in these offices have considerable responsibilities and they work under formal conditions of complete equality with men. So in the offices greater mutual adjustment by both men and women is necessary to enable women to play their appropriate roles without consideration of sex. Contrary to their traditional attitude towards women, men have to admit the latter's equality, being their colleagues and sometimes superiors. In recent years, women have done well in jobs including administrative ones. (Report of the committes on the status of women, 1974, 1989).

Men may not be prepared to accept a woman even as an equal let alone as a superior. At best, they may be prepared to accept a woman as an equal, but they may not relish working under a woman boss or taking orders from her. The career experience of men and women may well differ not only because the two groups differ in attitudes and aspirations but also because men and women are treated differently by society.

Accordingly, this book seeks to enquire into the performance of women administrators in offices, i.e., how well do they appear to perform their role in equality with males and how comfortable do they feel in the office, the reasons for taking the job, the respondents' opinion about the nature of the job, their job satisfaction, etc.

In Table 2.1, the administrators' reasons for taking job is given. 6.25% of the respondents took the job for economic reasons. For them, government service was the only way to get ahead and make both ends meet. Most executives (62.5%) were career ambitious. Since the service represented the highest attainment with academic qualification, they were attracted by the prestige, the prospects, the social position, and comforts it could bring. This category did not have any economic liabilities. For some administrators (12.5%) the reason for taking jobs was their desire to serve the poor and the needy. They were able to help many citizens every day who came to them seeking governments' help. They proved themselves to be true public servants. Few (12.5%) took the job mainly for improving their standard of living. Those families who were not very rich and for those people who wanted to provide for additional amenities for daily life, women have had to take up a job which they would not have taken otherwise. Since the services were taken up the by middle-class people, there were no respondents who felt that their job would prevent boredom. Many studies conducted by foreign sociologists showed that together with economic factors other factors were also responsible for women started working outside. Zweig[6] in 1952 found that economic pressure was the major factor. Margot Jeffreys[7] in a study of professionally qualified women working in the British Civil Service and other government agencies found that only 1 in 5 gave economic necessity as the main reason and their other reasons were extremely varied. Women with children gave dislike of domesticity as the main reason for taking up a job. According to Hannah Gavrou[8] although economic factors were the most important reasons for working, the next was a combination of boredom and loneliness.

Table 2.1. Reasons for Taking the Job

Reasons	% of response
Economic reason	6.25
Career ambition	62.50
Social Service	12.50
Better standard of living	12.50
Prevents boredom	-
No response	6.25
Total	100.00

Job Satisfaction

Majority of the administrators (68.75%) considered their job satisfactory and 25% of them felt it to be most satisfactory. There were none who could say that their job was not satisfactory. Therefore it could be said that almost all the administrators were satisfied with the nature of their job. Similarly

Chaturvedi's[9] findings also reveal that 91.7% executive and 85.9% educationists were satisfied with the nature of their job.

In Table 2.2a, the comparison between experience and job satisfaction is shown. From the Table it is clear that those respondents who were most satisfied with the nature of their job were found both among the less and more experienced administrators. Most of the women administrators interviewed described the administrative profession in very favourable terms and looked forward to increasing career responsibilities. Some even said that they seemed to be happy and content in their job. Some even said that they readily accepted and worked under any type of situation because it was their duty to do so. They willingly obeyed the government orders and executed them. Thus from the above analysis it could be derived that women in administrative services are fully satisfied with their jobs. This in turn, means that satisfied employees are more likely to show better output and higher level of performance. It would enable them to execute government policies in an efficient and effective manner.

Table 2.2a. Job Satisfaction

Job Satisfaction	Experience in Years						Total
	upto 5	5-10	10-15	15-20	20-25	above 25	
Satisfactory	6.25	18.75	18.75	6.25	6.25	12.50	68.75
Most satisfactory	-	6.25	-	6.25	12.50	-	25.00
Not Satisfactory	-	-	-	-	-	-	-
No response	-	-	-	6.25	-	-	6.25
Total%	6.25	25.00	18.75	18.75	18.75	12.50	100.00

All values are in %

Table 2.2b shows details about job satisfaction and the reasons for taking the job. It is clearly shown that all those who wanted to join the service with career ambition or to do social service and to have better standards of living were really satisfied. Few of the respondents who chose the job for career ambition were even most satisfied. This would definitely help the administrators to achieve the goals and challenges posed for them and this in turn would improve the efficiency and effectiveness of the Indian administrative system.

Table 2.2b. Job Satisfaction and the Reasons for Taking the Job

Job Satis-faction	Reasons						
	Economic reasons	Career ambition	Social service	Better standard	Prevent boredom	No response	Total
Satisfactory	-	37.50	12.50	12.50	-	6.25	68.75
Most Satisfactory	-	25.00	-	-	-	-	25.00
Not Satisfactory	-	-	-	-	-	-	-
No response	6.25	-	-	-	-	-	6.25
Total	6.25	62.50	12.50	12.50	-	6.25	100.00

All values are in %

Workload

According to the Table 2.3a 31.25% of the administrators, the workload was excessive. However, the majority of the respondents (62.5%) felt the workload was moderate. It was generally stated that they cope with the work and responsibilities assigned to them without difficulty. But those who felt their workload to be excessive complained that they had no free time to relax.

In Table 2.3a experience and workload are shown. The respondents' opinion about the workload was found to vary irrespective of the number of years in experience. There were respondents with same number of years experience who differed in their opinion about workload. Even though most of the administrators had more than five years of experience still some of them felt that their workload was excessive.

Table 2.3 a. Experience and Workload

Years	Work load				
	Excessive	Moderate	Less than Moderate	No Response	Total
Up to 5	-	6.25	-	-	6.25
5-10	6.25	18.75	-	-	25.00
10-15	12.00	6.25	-	-	18.75
15-20	6.25	6.25	-	6.25	18.75
20-25	6.25	12.50	-	-	18.75
above 25	-	12.50	-	-	12.50
Total	31.25	62.50	-	6.25	100.00

All values are in %

Similarly, comparison of job satisfaction with workload is given in Table 2.3b. It is known that majority of the respondents who felt the workload was excessive were found to be satisfied with their jobs. Whereas the majority of the respondents who found their job most satisfactory found that their workload was moderate and not excessive. Therefore it could be stated that when the officials felt their workload to be excessive then they would not find their job very interesting but when they found their work load was moderate they were much happier and satisfied with their jobs. Since there is a possibility that administrators could lose their efficiency if they feel discontented with their jobs, they should be strongly motivated for ensuring administrative effectiveness. They should be given some kind of incentive in the form of promotions. It should be granted strictly on the basis of merit rather than seniority. Then the efficiency of civil servants would improve.

Table 2.3b. Job Satisfaction and Workload

Job Satisfaction	Work load				
	Excessive	Moderate	Less than Moderate	No response	Total
Satisfactory	25.00	43.25	-	-	68.75
Most Satisfactory	6.25	18.75	-	-	25.00
Not Satisfactory	-	-	-	-	-
No Response	-	-	-	6.25	6.25
Total	31.25	62.50	-	6.25	100.00

All values are in %

Work after Office Hours

The number of administrators who sit behind to complete the work after the office hours was found. The result was that nearly 68.75% of the respondents responded affirmatively to that question. However, about 25% of the responded negatively. It shows that majority of the respondents were very dutiful and career oriented. As the nature of work done by civil servants is very important, they are responsible for the execution of the law passed by the legislature. The civil servants not only exercise control over the policies both before and after they are formed but also help the ministers in discharging their duties. They provide the skeleton within which the policies are formulated. They sometimes even legislate by framing regulation and issuing ordinances. That is why the civil servants are sometimes termed as "statesman in disguise". Therefore it is very essential that they must be efficient, impartial and competent. It is generally said that it will be a better guarantee for good government than a good constitution. In fact, in the absence of "an efficient body of administrators even the best of the constitutions is likely to be reduced to the position of a scrap of paper". But on the other hand an efficient body of civil servants can run the administration very efficiently in spite of certain draw backs in the constitution.

From Table 2.4 it is clear that both those respondents who stayed after office hours to complete their work as well as those who were not satisfied with their job. This shows that they were satisfied and very responsible towards their job.

Table 2.4. Job Satisfaction and Work After Office Hours

Job Satisfaction	Work load			
	Yes	No	No Response	Total
Satisfactory	50.00	18.75		68.45
Most Satisfactory	18.75	6.25	-	25.00
Not Satisfactory	-	-	-	-
No response	-	-	6.25	6.25
Total	68.75	25.00	6.25	100.00

All values are in %

Pending Files

The administrators were asked about taking work home. About 31.25% of the respondents frequently carried pending files home. There were nearly 56.25% of the administrators who occasionally took work home. However, there were also 6.25% of them who never took work home.

According to the Table 2.5a the experience of the administrators was related to their willingness to take pending files home. An attempt was made to find out if the respondents differed in their style of working as they put in more years of service. As experience increases there is a tendency of people working in government services to be slack in their style of working. They don't tend to work consistently. But this is not true in the case of administrators. Irrespective of their experience in the services, they carried the pending files home either frequently or occasionally.

Table 2.5a. Experience and Pending files

Years	Pending Files				
	Frequently	Occasionally	Never	No Response	Total
upto 5	-	6.25	-	-	6.25
5-10	-	25.00	-	-	25.00
10-15	18.75	-	-	-	18.75
15-20	-	12.50	-	6.5	18.75
20-25	6.25	6.25	6.25	-	18.75
above 25	6.25	6.25	-	-	12.50
Total	31.25	56.25	6.25	6.25	100.00

All values are in %

Table 2.5b shows the respondents' views on taking pending files home. Those who were satisfied with their job took the pending files either frequently or occasionally, and those who were most satisfied carried them occasionally or never took them home. Though the women administrators had to take home pending files occasionally they were all satisfied with their work. This is because the civil servants did not expect any publicity for good work done. They must rest content with the consciousness of good work done honestly.

Table 2.5b. Administrators' Views on Taking Pending Files

Job Satisfaction	Taking Pending Files				
	Frequently	Occasionally	Never	No Response	Total
Satisfactory	31.25	37.50	-	-	68.75
Most Satisfactory	-	18.75	6.25	-	25.00
Not Satisfactory	-	-	-	-	-
No Response	-	-	-	6.25	6.25
Total	31.25	56.25	6.25	6.25	100.00

However, in spite of their sincerity, civil servants in India are considered inferior in their standards, and slow moving as compared with their counterparts elsewhere. This is mainly due to mass recruitment after independence and excessive red-tapism, the habit of shirking responsibility and corruption. They adopted a long and dilatory procedure for reaching any decision.[10] It is therefore very desirable that the procedures be simplified to eliminate unnecessary delay. To eliminate the evil of corruption not only the economic but also the moral standards of the people must be raised. The above discussion clearly shows that the relationship existing between the ministers and the civil servants in India has not been very satisfactory and there is scope for improvement on both the sides.

Suggestions to Superiors

The nature of human interactions is influenced by social definitions as well as by the positions the interacting persons occupy. Though the women executives occupy lower positions than their bosses yet they are placed quite high in the organisational hierarchical set up. Further, they have come to occupy such a position based on their qualifications and experience and as such are expected to express their points of view to their bosses without any inhibition[11].

The civil servants must particularly cultivate the qualities of initiative, enterprise, originality, human understanding, and democratic contact. They are the executors of social reforms and they must therefore exhibit vitality, drive, initiative imagination. They must think carefully and act promptly and courageously.

Even though the civil servants are expected to give suggestions to their superiors, a study was made to find out if the women administrators did so or if they shirked responsibilities because of their sex. The results revealed that 87.5% of the respondents gave suggestions to their superiors while 12.5% of them did not respond to that question. Those who gave suggestions to superiors felt that they were bold and imaginative enough to plan things properly and manage affairs efficiently.

Difficulty in Working with Male Superiors

Women in a traditional society have lower status than men, and employment of women is an aberration to be tolerated for reasons of expediency rather than to be accepted as legitimate. The treatment, the women employees get from their superiors is an indicator of the pattern of discriminations or otherwise shown to them. If they get due respect, this may be considered as an indicator of men's recognition of their capacity of equal work.[12]

According to the findings the majority of the women administrators (93.75%) did not have any difficulty in working with male superiors. Only 6.25% found it difficult working with them. They too must be prepared to take decisions and shoulder responsibility.

In Table 2.6 religion and difficulty in working with male superiors is given. It is clear that only the Hindu respondents faced difficulty. The traditional custom of not relating with male members freely would have hindered them. This shows a negative value in the mind of Hindu women administrators.

Table 2.6. Religion and Difficulty in Working with Male Superiors

Religion	Difficulty with Male Superiors			
	Yes	No	No Response	Total
Hindu	6.25	68.75	-	75.00
Muslim	-	12.50	-	12.50
Christian	-	12.50	-	12.50
Others	-	-	-	-
Total	6.25	93.75	-	100.00

Difficulty in Working with Male Colleagues

Human groups are founded to satisfy the needs of the members, the essence of group life is cooperative interaction and mutual understanding among the members. The members of a peer group have almost the same status. They interact with each other as equals. They cooperate for their own good as well as for the organisation in which they work. As the members of a peer group are almost equal to each other, they are expected to plan their actions together and for the attainment of common goals. They are required to coordinate their activities.[13] To find out the extent of unity among the administrators including their male colleagues, the respondents were asked if they had any difficulty in working with male colleagues. Almost all (93.75%) of the respondents did not find any difficulty in working with their male counterparts. However, 6.25% of them did find it difficult to work with males.

Table 2.7 shows that only a few Hindu respondents found difficulty in working with male colleagues. This tendency is again due to the Indian culture among the Hindus inhibiting free interactions with males. This shows that the respondents suffered from some type of inferiority complex.

Table 2.7. Religion and Difficulty in Working with Male Colleagues

Religion	Difficulty with Male Superiors			
	Yes	No	No Response	Total
Hindu	6.25	68.75	-	75.00
Muslim	-	12.50	-	12.50
Christian	-	12.50	-	12.50
Others	-	-	-	-
Total	6.25	93.75	-	100.00

All the values are in %

Difficulty in Working with Male Subordinates

It is generally demanded that the officials should maintain a reasonable distance from their subordinates. If they become friendly with the subordinates, they would neither be able to get the work done nor would they be able to exercise authority over them. It was found that none of the respondents found any difficulty in working with male subordinates. This shows that women administrators knew how to relate with their subordinates and their authority helped them to get the work done from the subordinates. As per Table 2.8, it is clear that even the Hindu respondents did not find any difficulty in working with male subordinates.

Table 2.8. Religion and Working with Male Subordinates

Religion	Difficulty with male Superiors			
	Yes	No	No Response	Total
Hindu	-	75.00	-	75.00
Muslim	-	12.50	-	12.50
Christian	-	12.50	-	12.50
Others	-	-	-	-
Total	-	100.00	-	100.00

All the values are in %

Thus from the above analysis it is clear that the process of modernisation in India has been set in motion in the recent past. However, it does not mean that Indian women have completely discarded their traditional value system. Even though they are following Western societies in regard to education, new technology, production, relations, they are also retaining their Hindu cultural traits of not relating freely with male members. This depicts the lower status of women even among the highly educated administrators.

Suffered Due to Discrimination of Sex

Several reports exist, of discrimination against women in the higher services. Discrimination may exist in the nationalised corporations or within certain state administrations. Whatever the actual extent of discrimination in the higher services, most women administrators want to convey the idea that they are competent professionals and are treated as such.

According to the findings 93.75% of the women administrators felt that they did not suffer from discrimination of sex. However, 6.25% felt that they were discriminated against because they were women. Hence it could be said that even though women administrators claimed to be equal to their male counterparts still, women in civil services suffered from sex discrimination.

Suffered Due to Discrimination of Caste

Caste as a system of social relations has been a central point in the Hindu society for several years. A caste is an endogamous group, that is, its members marry within the caste. A man is born in a caste and remains in that forever. Members of a caste used to have a particular occupation on a hereditary basis. A given caste occupies a particular rank in the hierarchy of castes, hence some are superior and some are inferior. At the top are Brahmanas and at the bottom are the 'untouchable castes'. There are certain rules regarding eating, drinking and social interaction which are to be followed by all the castes. Caste is a dynamic institution, it has changed a great deal in accordance with changes in the wider Indian society.[14]

In this study the women administrators were asked if they suffered due to discrimination of caste. Most of them (93.75%) felt that they did not suffer due to discrimination of caste. This was mainly because it was common for most of the women administrators to choose their husbands from other castes who were in the same professions. Hence caste did not play a major role in their lives. Moreover, education has helped them to build the bridge between superior caste and inferior caste. Therefore all were considered equals irrespective of their background of caste.

Suffered Due to Discrimination of Religion

Religion has played an important part in Indian society from the earliest times. It has assumed numerous forms and nomenclatures in relation to different groups of people associated with it. India is a multi-religious society. Transformation and changes in different religions have occurred from time to time with changes in intellectual climate and social structure. Religion in India has never been static. Today it has made inroads into the arenas of politics and economic life.

According to the findings only 6.25% of the administrators suffered from discrimination whereas most of them (93.75%) did not suffer discrimination due to religion.

Suffered Due to Discrimination of Language

The present formation of India into 'states' represents the language map of India. The States Reorganisation Commission (SRC) carved out states based on linguistic uniformity and continuity. It seems that the root cause of the present language problem is the imposition of English by the British Raj in India. Lord Macaulay said : "We must at present do our best to form a class who may be interpreters between us and the millions whom we govern; a class of persons, Indian in blood and colour, but English in taste, in opinions, in morals and in intellect". He continued : "To that class we may leave it to refine the vernacular dialects of the country, to enrich those dialects with terms by degrees fit vehicles for conveying knowledge to the great mass of the population.[15]

However, there is also a counter-view that India joined the world community through its English education. The promotion of vernaculars would have been a threat to India's unity. The study of science and technology was made possible by the knowledge of English. Even today English is considered a necessary licence to get lucrative and prestigious jobs. English has thus created a hiatus between the elite and the masses. On the other hand, the indigenous languages have received the attention required for preservation and enrichment. It brings about emotional integration and national consolidation. But this would be a direct attack on the small upper class entrenched in administration, law-enforcement professions, business and industry as their use of English as the basic instrument of communication. If indigenous language is used in administration and planning it may block proper communication between people speaking different 'national languages'. Inter language rivalries might also arise.

In this study the women administrators in Tamil Nadu were found to be proficient in the regional language (Tamil). Only a small group of 6.25% of the respondents suffered due to discrimination of language and majority of them about 93.75% did not have any difficulty in language. There have been sharp protests in non-Hindi speaking areas such as Andhra Pradesh, Tamil Nadu, Kerala, Karnataka, Bengal and Assam following advocation of Hindi as the official language. The administrators in order to be true public servants took the trouble of learning Tamil, the regional language for proper communication with the general masses. This problem could be solved if the three language formula is implemented which includes the study of modern Indian languages, preferably one of the southern languages apart from Hindi and English in the Hindi speaking states, and of Hindi along with the regional language and English in the non-Hindi speaking states.

Frequent Transfers Affects Efficiency

The relations between the civil servants and ministers is such that in India, influence and corruption play a significant role in the postings, transfers and promotions of civil servants. It is desirable that all appointments, promotions, postings and transfers should be on the grounds of merit, special aptitude, experience and in accordance with the seniority rules laid down so that the efficiency of administration can be retained.

The respondents were asked if frequent transfers affected their efficiency. According to 25% of the respondents frequent transfers affected their efficiency but nearly 56.25% of the respondents disagreed with the statement and about 18.75% of them did not respond to the question. Those who felt that their efficiency was not affected said that they were trained to work in all situations and therefore were prepared for transfers. However, there is a complaint in India that civil servants are becoming servile and there is too much interference in their official work. It is desirable that every effort should be made to preserve their independence and objective outlook. Ministers must resist the temptation to interfere in the day-to-day administration of a department. Members of legislature and party leaders who try to influence civil servants particularly at district level should be prevented from doing so.

Unpleasant Experiences in Service

The women administrators were asked to state whether they had any unpleasant experience in their service. It was found that none of the women administrators had any unpleasant experience. About 62.5% of them said they sometimes had, but nearly 31.25% said that they never experienced any unpleasant situation in their service.

Recommendation of Women to Join Civil Services

The women administrators were asked regarding recommendations of other women to join civil services. It was found that 87.5% of the respondents recommended women to join the services and 6.25% of them did not, 6.25% of them did not reply to the question. It could be said that they were not fully content with the nature of the job. Some felt that they suffered due to their sex. They were unable to cope with the hardships they had to undergo like their counterparts. Others felt it was tiresome and exhausting and they were unable to spend time with their family. Hence they felt that it was not advisable for women to join civil services for those women who wanted to fulfill their role even in their families.

Table 2.9 shows the relationship of the recommendations of women to join the civil services and job satisfaction. It is clear from the Table that all those women administrators who were either satisfied or most satisfied with their jobs had recommended other women to join the services and those who did not recommend women to the services were among those who did not talk about their job satisfaction. Therefore, it could be derived that those respondents who were not fully content or happy about their jobs did not recommend other women to join the civil services.

Table 2.9. Job satisfaction Vs Recommendation of Women Administrators to the service

Job satisfaction	Recommendation of women(%)			
	Yes	No	No response	Total
Satisfied	56.25	6.25	6.25	68.75
Most Satisfied	25.00	-	-	25.00
Not Satisfied	-	-	-	-
No Response	6.25	-	-	6.25
Total	87.50	6.25	6.25	100.00

Conclusion

There are several factors that seem to be associated with the general satisfaction of women in the elite administrative services. For most of the women administrators career ambition was the reason for taking the job while others took it either for economic reason or as a social service or to improve their standards of living. All the respondents were satisfied with their nature of the job, but some felt that the workload was excessive. Most of them were dutiful and stayed after office hours to complete their work and some of them took pending files home in order to complete their work.

The women administrators boldly gave suggestions to their superiors, most of them did not have any difficulty in working with male superiors, and almost all of them did not find any difficulty in working with male colleagues and subordinates.

Most of the women executives felt that they did not suffer due to sex discrimination, caste, religion, or language. A little more than fifty percent of the respondents disagreed with the view that frequent transfer affects efficiency while others agreed that it did affect their efficiency. There were some respondents who felt that they never had any unpleasant experiences in their service while some experienced them sometimes. However, majority of the respondents recommended other women to join civil services.

Notes and References

[1] Sengupta, Padmini, *Women Workers of India*, Bombay: Asia Publishing House, 1960, pp. 2-3.

[2] Everett, Jana, "Women in Law and Administration" in Everett.J, Lebra. J, and Paulson, J., ed., *Women and Work: Continuity and Change*, New Delhi: Promilla & Co. Publications, 1984, p. 239.

[3] Sahai, Nisha "Women in Administration: A Growing Phenomenon", Aijiet Cour, ed., *Directory of Indian Women Today*, New Delhi: India International Publishers, 1976, p. 25.

[4] Everett, Op. cit., p. 242.

[5] Mahajan, Amarjit, *Indian Police Women*, New Delhi: Deep and Deep Publications, 1982, pp. 34-35.

[6] Ferdyn and Zweig, *Women Life and Labour*, London: Gollanez, 1952.

[7] Jeffreys, Margot, "Married Women in the Higher Grades of Civil Service and Government Sponsored Research Organisations", *British Journal of Sociology*, Vol 3, no. 4, (1952), pp. 361-364.

[8] Goveru, Hannah, *The Captive Wife*, London: Routledge and Kegan Paul, 1966, pp.112 - 126.

[9] Chaturvedi, G., *Women Administrators of India*, Jaipur: RBSA Publications, 1985, p. 178.

[10] Srivastava, L.N., *Comparative Political Systems-Theory and Practice of Modern Government*, Fourth Revised Edition, Delhi: SBD Enterprises, 1988, pp. 269-282.

[11] Krisonswasdi, Napasri, *Women Executives – A Sociological Study in Role Effectiveness*, Jaipur: Rawat Publications, 1989, p. 178.
[12] Lalitha Devi, V., *Status and Employment of Women in India*, Delhi: B.R. Publishing Corporation, 1982, p. 95.
[13] Krisnoswasdi, Napasri, Op. cit., pp : 90-91.
[14] Sharma, K.L., "Indian Society", New Delhi: NCERT, 1990, p.87.
[15] Ibid p : 11.

3

Women Administrators at Home

Introduction

Family organisation forms the basic core of a given society's sexual division of labour, marital norms and a system of control over resources, rights, duties and privileges of the members. Significance of family for women is even more vital than for men, as one can talk of the social problems of the latter without involving the family, but for the former, one cannot speak about their social problems without dealing with their family functions. Motherhood is a supreme goal which is socially celebrated, and is to be undertaken within the domestic domain along with the experiences of work and leisure. While a man is allowed an independent existence, woman's survival is not socially conceivable without the family. The social value placed on the familial role of woman is also responsible for her lack of access to economic and political resources, even when she contributes equally or more to the family economy. Thus, while the family throttles women's aspirations towards positions of power and equality, it also places significant responsibilities on them and provides almost the only means of social survival in the majority of societies today.[1] American society considered that women cannot be good engineers or lawyers because these professions call for qualities which are not feminine.[2]

Accordingly in this chapter an attempt is made to study the household responsibilities and the time management of the women administrators and to analyse the status of women administrators within the family.

Number of Children

The respondents were asked about the number of children they had. The responses among the married administrators were categorised as no children, one child, two children and more than two. It was found that about 6.25% of the administrators had no children, 25% of them had one child and 43.75% of them had two children. There were 6.25% of them who had even more than two children. Those women administrators who had more than two children were found to be between the age brackets of 45-50 years. It was found that these women administrators did not have family planning measures when they were young which are improved and followed to a greater extent now. Hence it could be said that almost all the respondents followed family planning measures formulated by the Government.

Children's Position

The children of women administrators were studied in order to find out how many of them were young children and how many of them were grown ups. It was found that none of the administrators had children who were below school age. However, the majority of the respondents, about 68.75%, had children of school age and 6.25% of them had grown up children who were graduating. The respondents who had school children, were tossed between their responsibilities at home as mothers and those as executives at the office. Therefore, several questions were asked about their time management which are discussed below.

Care of Children

It is believed that mothers play a major role in the development of their children. Neglect or carelessness on their part may handicap the child physically, mentally or emotionally for the rest of the child's life. However, nowadays there is an increasing tendency on the part of many mothers to leave their children to the care of "*ayahs*" or servants and to concentrate either on their career or on earning additional income for the family. The effects of such neglect of the children are often seen only in later years when things become impossible to correct.

In this study the women administrators were asked about how they managed to take care of their children. It was found that nearly 31.25% of the administrators left their children with relations or servants and 43.75% of them left their children to be looked after by their husbands. Even though Tamil Nadu is traditional in its outlook, it was found that due to the circumstances where women worked outside their homes, even male members of the family had to share the work at home.

Women administrators obviously could not stay at home looking after their children. Therefore their husbands had to take care of their children. Since most of the respondents were living in a nuclear family, the care of children was a severe problem because there was no other member of the family with whom the children could be left. Hence in Table 3.3, a comparison of the type of family of the respondents is made with the care of children. The table shows that 25% of the respondents who lived in nuclear families left their children to the care of their relatives and servants whereas 37.5% of them had their husbands to do this. Whereas in the case of the respondents living in joint families 6.25% of them left their children with relations and 6.25% had their husbands to take care of the children. It was found that for the respondents who were living in a nuclear family were at a disadvantage because they could not leave their children with relations. They either had to leave them behind with their servants or their partners. The respondents who lived in joint families could leave their children with relations, or their partner instead of leaving the children at the mercy of servants. Their children would not be neglected even if their partners could not manage to look after them. Since most of the women administrators had partners in the same profession they too are expected to be busy and it would be difficult for their partners to look after their children. So the respondents in the nuclear families had to leave their children at the mercy of servants and therefore there were chances of their children being neglected.

Table 3.3. Family Type and Care of Children

Family Type	Care of Children				
	Alone	Relatives and Servants	Husbands	No Response	Total
Nuclear	-	25.00	37.50	25.00	87.50
Joint	-	6.25	6.25	-	12.50
No response	-	-	-	-	-
Total	-	31.25	43.75	25.00	100.00

Help to Children

Similarly, the respondents were asked to indicate whether they managed to help their children in their studies. Although women administrators were busy with their hectic work it is a surprise that still 6.25% of them managed to help their children. 6.25% of the respondents shared with relatives or servants and most of them nearly 62.5% had their husbands to help their children.

In Table 3.4 it is shown that those respondents who lived in nuclear families and could help their children in studies were about 6.25% and nearly 56.25% of them could not help them but left their children to be helped by their husbands. However, among those who lived in joint families, 6.25% had their relations to help their children, and about 6.25% of them left their children to be helped by their husbands. Thus it is clear that the respondents could not combine both the obligations of helping their children as well as being executives. They were fully dependent on others to fulfill their household responsibilities.

Table 3.4. Family type and Help to children

Family Type	Help to Children				
	Alone	Relatives and Servants	Husbands	No Response	Total
Nuclear	6.25	-	56.25	25.00	87.50
Joint	-	6.25	6.25	-	12.50
No response	-	-	-	-	-
Total	6.25	6.25	62.50	25.00	100.00

Purchase of Grocery

Food being essential for man to live, purchase of grocery becomes necessary and is mostly done by women. Keeping in view the respondents' nature of job they were asked if they purchase grocery. 12.5% of them managed to shop alone and 81.25% had their relations or servants to buy things and 6.25% of the respondents even sent their husbands to purchase grocery for their family. We find that in a nuclear family, it is always the partner and their children alone whereas there are more people in an extended family and they tend to share the responsibilities among themselves. An attempt was made to find out whether the respondents who managed to shop for grocery belonged only to nuclear families or also to joint families.

From Table 3.5 it is clear that 6.25% respondents who belonged to nuclear families could shop for grocery, whereas 75% of them had relatives and friends to do this. 6.25% of the respondents had their husbands to purchase grocery. 6.25% respondents who belonged to joint families shopped alone and 6.25% had their relatives and servants for this. Hence it is clear that some of the women executives did manage to shop for grocery while most of them could not.

Table 3.5 Family Type and Purchase of Grocery

Family Type	Purchase of Grocery				
	Alone	Relatives and Servants	Husbands	No Response	Total
Nuclear	6.25	75.00	6.25	-	87.50
Joint	6.25	6.25	-	-	12.50
No Response	-	-	-	-	-
Total	12.50	81.25	6.25	-	100.00

Cooking and Serving

In a traditional society of Tamil Nadu, the female member of the family, usually the wife, or in the case of a joint family the daughters-in-law are expected to cook and serve. However, in the changing modern society the working women do not find time and some do not enjoy cooking. They employ cooks as servants. Cooking is interesting for some and they manage to get the help of others in assisting them when they do not find enough time to do it alone. It was found that women administrators enjoyed cooking and 12.5% of them managed to cook alone without seeking other's help and most of them nearly 68.75% shared it with servants or relatives and about 6.25% shared with their husbands.

In Table 3.6 it is clear that those respondents who managed to cook alone and also those who took the help of their husbands were only from the nuclear families. It is obvious that due to the nature of their job and existing situations they had to do all by themselves or seek their partners help. But the respondents belonging to joint families could always get the help from other women in the family. There was no need for them to even employ a cook. Therefore, it could be said that most of the women executives did not find time to cook or serve. They had to share the responsibility with their husbands or employ a cook in the case of nuclear family and if they lived in a joint family it was done by relatives or other women in the family.

Table 3.6 Family Type and Cooking and Serving

Family Type	Cooking and Serving				
	Alone	Relatives and Servants	Husbands	No Response	Total
Nuclear	12.50	68.75	6.25	-	87.50
Joint	-	12.50	-	-	12.50
No Response	-	-	-	-	-
Total	12.50	81.25	6.25	-	100.00

Care of Sick

When both the spouses are working as administrators in a family it becomes difficult to look after sick people at home. Since most of the respondents belonged to nuclear families usually it would be their own children and therefore they would find it very difficult to leave them when sick to the care of their servants. Moreover, as it was found that majority of the respondents had school children and not grown ups, the respondents were asked to indicate what adjustments they made during times of illness. In Table 3.7, the various responses of the respondents are presented. About 6.25% of them said that they managed to look after the sick all by themselves and 37.50% of them had relations or servants. Nearly 43.75% of the respondents shared the responsibility with their husbands. As it is impossible for the partners to have rigid types of duties, they had to be flexible in sharing their domestic responsibilities with mutual adjustment and understanding. Only then could they have peaceful, happy and enjoyable lives. Table 3.7b is self-explanatory. The respondents of nuclear family were the ones who looked after the sick alone, or shared with their husbands and servants because there was no other possibility. In the case of the respondents in joint families they could leave their sick children with other members of the family. It is difficult to find servants who are trustworthy in the absence of members of the family.

Table 3.7 Family Type Compared with Care of Sick

Family Type	Care of sick				
	Alone	Relatives and Servants	Husbands	No Response	Total
Nuclear	6.25	31.25	37.50	12.50	87.50
Joint	-	6.25	6.25	-	12.50
No Response	-	-	-	-	-
Total	6.25	37.50	43.75	12.50	100.00

Working Women and Neglect of Home

As working women are usually blamed for neglecting their domestic responsibilities in not fulfilling their obligations to their husbands and children. The children tend to suffer from lack of affection and love. The respondents were asked if they were guilty of causing such feelings or whether they felt that they could manage being executives and mothers to their children or wife to their partners without neglecting either of the duties.

It was found that 43.75% of the respondents did confess that they neglected their responsibilities at home. About 31.25% did not accept the statement. However, 25% of the respondents did not want to comment on the statement. All those who felt guilty for neglecting their families said that they enjoyed their prestigious profession which they achieved with considerable effort and they could not afford to quit it. All those who said that they were not guilty of neglecting the family, had prepared their children psychologically and also their husbands to being aware of their nature of duties. So they could work, give justice to their jobs and simultaneously share their love and affection with their children.

It is always not true that all housewives are able to give full attention to their children. They too are engaged in their housework. They too feel tired of doing household work all the time. They look for some outlet or get engaged in some social activity outside their homes. There is every possibility for a housewife to neglect the family. Hence it could be said that it is not true that working women neglect home and housewives are super mums. There has to be flexibility in sex roles in carrying the duties and sharing the responsibilities between both the partners, women executives being no exception.

Tradition of Females Eating after Males

Women are considered as subordinate subjects in society. They are expected to treat men of the family with respect and therefore the tradition of females eating only after males is followed even in Tamil Nadu like any other part of India. The elderly women or the mothers in the house train the young girls in the family that they should always first serve the men in the family and then eat themselves.

The women executives were asked if the tradition of females eating after males was followed in their family. None of the respondents always followed the tradition. About 6.25% of them sometimes followed when they had many family members gathering for any occasion. However, most of the executives, 93.75% said that they never followed it. Therefore, it is clear from the analysis that the tradition of lowering the status of women has not been fully eradicated from the society. Even though women have entered almost all the fields open to men, they are still considered as second class citizens and lower to men. This attitude should be changed by educating both men and women to the view that they are partners in everything, to share and care for one another. Only then will women be accepted as equal to men.

It was found that the roots of traditional values in the society are deep and therefore the practice of restricting women on mingling with others during menstruation is still followed in some of the families of women executives. Since women were considered as untouchables and impure during menstruation they were not allowed to move freely during menstruation. This practice is still followed in many educated families. However, the age old customs like female members not standing in the presence of male members, separate apartments for women, restriction on the freedom of movement of women outside the family and entertaining or receiving friends are not followed any longer due to the modernisation and the changes in society. Therefore change in society has to some extent change the people's attitudes.

Preferential Treatment to Boys

Another intolerable affront to the dignity of a woman is the deep-seated cultural value of giving preference to the male child. The preference for the male child, so widely entertained by both men and women, can also be traced to domestic and marital practices. The domestic tradition of sons staying with their parents automatically leads to the custom of aged parents living with their son's family and not with the daughter's. The practice gives one the impression that sons are needed for security in old age, putting into the background the fact that the son inherits the lions share of the parent's property. Again it is the son who emerges as the supporter of the widowed mother, because the practice for a man to almost invariably marry a younger woman. That is why women paves the way for most women to live a life of widowhood relatively at an early age and are even crazier than men, in their desire for male children. The Hindu custom of sons lighting the pyre of the parents also encourages preferential treatment to boys. The women administrators were asked to respond whether they gave preferred treatment to boys than girls. About 6.25% of the respondents felt preferential treatment was given to boys in their families. However, 93.75% of them felt that they were treated as equals. But when they were asked whether they would still follow the tradition of giving their daughters in marriage to older men, they said that they would continue to do so.

So it appears that the exaggerated preference for the male child would continue so long as the present practices of living arrangements and of marrying younger wives go unchecked. But the inordinate desire for male child poses a threat not only to the status of women, but to the very survival of girl babies especially in the context of the small family norm. Most surveys of fertility behaviour, these days show that while people desire smaller families, the ideal composition of the family preferred by most couples consists of two sons and a daughter. But in practice, parents who desire a small family, complete their family when the quota of desired number of sons is fulfilled even though the quota of daughters is not filled. On the other hand, if the quota of sons is not filled even though the desired size of the family is attained, they do not mind enlarging the family size even when there are more daughters than the desired number. What is worse is that with easy accessibility to the facilities of amniocentesis and abortion, they simply do away with the female foetus. Therefore, it is high time that women executives as policy makers pay serious attention to this alarming trend in the sex ratio which is damaging both to the existence of women and the well-being of the society.

Time to Entertain Guests and Relatives

Administrators occupied with official matters, hardly have any time to spare for their family, friends and relatives. But, south India is basically renowned for its hospitality. Women follow the tradition of welcoming their guests by offering water to anyone who comes to the home as a token of acceptance of that person into the family. They spend time with guests and make them feel at home. They then try to entertain them in whatever way possible.

Table 3.8. Time to entertain guest and relatives

Answers	%
Yes	56.25
No	43.75
No Response	-
Total	100.00

There is also a tradition of welcoming the related couples who are newly weds and offering them some gifts or clothes. There are other occasions where the families get together and enjoy having fun. Even though they stay as nuclear families they are still closely knitted with their family and friends. In this context the respondents were asked if as administrators with heavy responsibilities and duties they could find time to entertain their guests and relatives at home. It was found that 56.25% of them really could entertain guests with their tight schedule and 43.75% of them said that they could not afford to entertain anyone at home due to lack of time. The responses can be seen in Table 3.8. Therefore from the above findings it could be said that the respondents were conscious of their position in the government and were devoted to their job at the expense of their families. They would forego anything for the sake of their job. Some felt that they wanted to join others, but could not, whereas others simply did not want to get closer with others as it was time-consuming. There were some who even felt that as the extremists increased in the state, it was dangerous to mingle with the public. It is true that the lives of administrators are always at risk it they are conscientious in their job: in implementing policies: simply in not dancing according to the tune played by politicians. They could be attacked by 'nasty' elements incited by political support.

Spending Leisure Time

From the study it is clear that women administrators mostly did not find time for anything other than their job. They were asked to explain how they spent their leisure time. About 12.5% of them spent their leisure time in some kind of entertainment, while 43.75% of them spent time in visiting friends and another 43.75% of them spent time in reading magazines, books and daily newspapers both national and international.

Magazines

The respondents were asked to mention the different types of magazines they read. In Table 3.9 it is seen that 43.75% of them read only national magazines like *Reader's Digest*, *Illustrated Weekly*, *Femina*, *Eve's Weekly*, *Economic Times* and *Savvy* and 56.25% of them read both local and national magazines. The local magazines being *Kalki*, *Kumudam* and *Ananda Vigadan* amongst others.

Table 3.9. Magazines

	%
National	43.75
Both local and national	56.25
No response	-
Total	100.00

Those respondents who read only national magazines were not natives of Tamil Nadu. They came from other parts of the country to serve as women administrators in Tamil Nadu and they said that even though they could read Tamil they were not interested in the magazines in Tamil. It shows that language was still a barrier for the women administrators even though they worked in the state for several years. It would therefore seem appropriate that the three language formula be followed in all educational systems and working institutions to encourage unity in diversity.

Newspapers

The respondents were asked whether they read only national or both local and national newspapers. As seen earlier the respondents whose mother tongue was other than Tamil preferred national newspapers like the *Hindu, Indian Express* and *Sunday Times*, whereas they sometimes read the local newspapers also in order to be aware of local happenings. Some read local daily papers to improve their vocabulary in Tamil. Around 37.5% of them preferred only national newspapers, while 62.5% of them read both local and national newspapers.

Conclusion

The study of women administrators' role at home shows that most of the married respondents had children and the majority of them had school children. The respondents could not take care of the children. They left their children either with servants or their husbands because they were in nuclear families. Those in the joint families left their children with their relations. Most of the respondents could not even help their children in their studies. Purchase of grocery, cooking and serving could not be done.

Sometimes some of them managed to do the household responsibilities with the help of their servants or husbands in the family. Since most of the respondents were living as nuclear families usually when their children were sick they could not leave their children to the care of their servants. Therefore, some of them did manage to take care of the sick all by themselves while others left them with their husbands or relations.

Evaluating their conditions, the women administrators were asked to comment on the statement "working women tend to neglect their homes". In response to the statement nearly 50% of them accepted that their families were neglected because they could not do justice to both their responsibilities at home and at the office. Some of them said that they could cope with both their duties without neglecting either of them. But there had to be flexibility in the roles of partners in sharing their duties in order to have a happy home. When one partner had to be away from home then the other partner would be able to manage the responsibilities at home and vice versa.

Tamil Nadu has a tradition where the females usually eat only after serving the male members of the family. In some families the respondents followed the tradition depending upon the situation. If at a family get-together there were many members present they served the males first. The majority of the respondents felt that they never followed the tradition in their families. In some of the families women were not allowed to mingle with others during menstruation. Therefore it is clear that women are still considered as second class citizens in some families even though they hold high posts as administrators.

Another deep-seated culture of giving preferential treatment to boys is still followed in Tamil Nadu in some families of the respondents but the majority of them said that they gave equal treatment to the sexes. This should be controlled by paying attention to the fertility treatment and amniocentesis available for the people.

More than fifty percent of the respondents felt that they could afford to entertain their friends and guests at home in spite of their office responsibilities. However, some of them could not do this because they did not find time while few of them did not want to get closer with others simply because they were afraid of trusting anyone. This fear could be removed if the interference of the politicians unnecessarily in the matters of administration is checked or is controlled. Both the politicians and administrators have to function smoothly hand in hand.

Finally it was found that language was still a barrier to some of the non-Tamil speaking respondents. Therefore the need for implementing the three language formula in education and working institutions is recommended.

Notes and References

[1] Desai, Neera & Maithreyi, Krishnaraj, *Women and Society in India*, Delhi: Ajanta Publications, 1987, pp. 184-185.
[2] Epstein, Cynthia Fuchs, *Women's Place, Options & Limits in Professional Careers*, University of California Press, 1973, p. 152.

4

Attitudes towards Social Change

Introduction

From the early times, attitude towards women was not in equal terms with men though women played distinctive roles as court poetess, inventors, political leaders and participated in decision-making bodies like panchayats and councils. The differentiation between male and female is seen at every level. Certainly the dissimilarity starts at home. The joy at the birth of a boy child is absent when a girl child is born. Often the mother herself discriminates against the girl child. This perspective is developed and rooted as norms to be followed by girls and women in their lives.[1]

The International Women's Decade came to an end in 1985 witnessing a series of conferences, seminars, action programmes, emergence of women's organisations and women's movements against atrocities meted out to women in all stages and areas in their life. There is a widespread awareness of women's life conditions and problems and issues faced by them in almost all the corners' of the world, and India being no exception.

However, a persistent worry and fear come at our heart as we witness increasing incidents of violence against women, which are regularly highlighted by newspapers. Almost every day there is news about bride burning, suicide, rape, abduction, eve-teasing, female infanticide.

Recently there are constant reports on sex determination tests of foetus, resulting in innumerable cases of aborting female foetus.[2]

One could go on counting such incidents for ages. According to various women's organisations an equal number of burning/suicide cases go unreported. Mostly this is on account of the refusal of the police to register the cases. Even when they do register, they tend to underplay the offense. For example over 90% of the cases of women burnt in Delhi were registered as accidents, only 5% were noted as murders and 5% as suicides.[3]

The dowry witch-hunt has taken its heaviest toll in the middle-class urban areas, but the burning of women for more money and domestic goods in the form of dowry is quite widespread in the slums and rural areas. Investigations have indicated that women burning is prevalent all over the country.

The atrocities committed against women within families have often been hidden from the public eye by a social attitude which is a mix of apathy towards women and an inexplicable sense of privacy.[4]

Need for Social Change

Social change is initiated in the structure and culture of society. The structure of society refers to infrastructural facilities, their distribution among people and also people's access to them. The culture of society consists of tradition, religion and norms of living and behaving with each other. Since the structure and culture of society have not remained static, therefore social change becomes an inevitable process. It is always for a better prospect. As both tradition and modernity coexist continuity and change have become empirical facts of social life. Tradition and continuity coexist, because all societies need a certain amount of stability and social checks. Modernity and change are required to attain new levels of knowledge and technical know-how to meet the changing demands and challenges. It is these conditions which call for social change.[5]

Education and Attitudes

Education equips the individual with traditions, customs, language habits, skills, beliefs and attitudes. In its knowledge and character building, education inculcates theoretical and practical realisation of values in the individual by developing physical and mental skills, perception, memory, comprehension, thinking attitudes and values. Attitudes, values and ideals, that are propagated by education play a significant role, in building the personality, individually and the entire mental make-up of an individual. Attitudes are the prime movers of thought and action. What a women thinks, feels and values are reflected in her expressed attitudes that are to be transmitted to the coming generations.[6] Hence this chapter highlights the attitudes of women administrators towards social change. The views of the respondents have been taken into account to know if they consciously work for the upliftment of the women. Their attitudes towards the women's right to property, dowry system, casteism, type of marriage and family, remarriage of widows, minimum age of marriage for a girl, importance of education and employment and various social problems are studied.

Treatment of Men and Women as Equals

Women's quest for equality with men has become universal. It has given birth to women's movements and feministic activities and associations. All over the world, feminism has its origin in social structure. Several constraints such as inequalities between men and women and discrimination against women, have been age old issues. For a long time women remained within the four walls of their households. Their dependence on men folk was total. Educated women in particular and the poor ones in general realised the need for taking up employment outside the household. Within the household, women have demanded equality with men, what exists for men is demanded for women. Today women organisations, women social workers and politicians have taken up issues like price-rise, dowry, rape, exploitation, etc. Women have demanded their share of jobs in the police and other such services. Women organisations have created a sense of consciousness for gender equality particularly in the urban areas.

Therefore, the respondents were asked to comment on the statement – "Men and women should be treated as equals". In Table 4.1, 68.75% of the women agreed with the statement and 31.25% of them strongly agreed, and none disagreed with the statement. This shows that the respondents being educated women, understood the existing problem of gender inequality and therefore positively confirmed that both men and women should be treated as equals.

Table 4.1 : Men and Women as Equals

Agree	68.75%
Strongly Agree	31.25%
Disagree	-
Strongly Disagree	-
Uncertain	-
Total	100.00%

In free India, trust, justice, equality and fraternity are the four pillars on which the constitution and our policy rests. Many of the ideals enshrined in the directive principles have been translated into reality by the central government. The Equal Remuneration Act has assured equal pay to men and women for work of equal value. The government has launched upon an ambitious programme to eradicate female illiteracy by 2000 AD.[7]

Therefore, as women administrators they would consciously work for the upliftment of the status of women in India. Policies and legislation to eliminate discrimination and promote equal sharing of responsibilities between women and men have not yet become a reality in many countries. It was noted that the United Nations' Convention on the "Elimination of All Forms of Discrimination Against Women" has still not been ratified by a large number of countries.[8]

Men and Women Should Have Equal Right to Property

Though men and women have equal rights to property according to Hindu law, in reality women remain in an inferior position so far as her rights to property and inheritance under different laws are concerned. The differentiation between sons and daughters becomes evident in the context of joint family property. Under Hindu law joint families follow two schools of thought. The Dayabhaga School gives importance to the father and holds that during the father's life, the sons, grandsons and great grandsons who constitute the joint family together with the father have no right to property and their rights remain only to one of the expectancies. According to the Mitakshara School, the joint family has a small nucleus known as coparcenary, of which no women can be a member, and it is composed of the father and his descendants of male line. The right of a member of the coparcener is a right by birth.

Muslim law discriminates between male and female heirs giving women the right to inherit only half the share of property when compared to men.

The Christians in Kerala were governed by the Travancore Christian Succession Act, 1916, and the Cochin Christian Succession Act, 1921. Apart from multiplicity, these laws give only a life interest terminable on death or remarriage to a widow or mother inheriting immovable property. A daughter's right is limited to "Stridhanam" and had limited her share to Rs. 500/-. As per the Indian Succession Act regarding the property of an intestate Indian Christian, the widow will inherit 1/3 of his properties and the children will take the remaining. If there are no children, the widow will get 1/2 of the property and the other half shall go to the distant kindred. If in case there are no kindred the whole of the property will go to the widow. When the intestate has left no widow and no other relatives, the property will go to the government.[9]

In Goa, the widow is relegated to the fourth position and is entitled to only fruits and agricultural commodities. In Pondicherry, the law relegate a women to an inferior position and do not regard her as full owner even in the few cases where she can inherit property.

For intestate succession among Parsees, the rules of devolution of property of male and female intestates differ, resulting in discrimination against daughters and mothers. The son is entitled to an equal share in the mother's property along with a daughter but the daughter is not entitled to the same right to the father's property. There is no justification for such discrimination.[10]

When the respondents were specifically asked to react to the statement that 'Men and Women should have equal rights in property,' 31.25% of them agreed and 62.5% of them strongly agreed and there were also 6.25% of them who also disagreed with the statement. There was a small number of women administrators who felt there is no need for women to claim equal share in property. Those who took this stand felt that the age old traditions should be broken and if it was done then there will be strained relationships between the children. Secondly, the parents and brothers fulfill their responsibility of giving away the daughters and sisters in marriage by borrowing heavy amounts to be given either in the form of gifts of dowry. Thirdly, they felt that their parents were the best judge to divide their property among children and their rights in this matter should not be questioned.

However, those respondents who supported the statement reasoned out that if the parental property was equally divided between the children then there was no need for the parents or brothers to worry about the marriage expenditure or to become bankrupt. They could spend on each child out of their share and thus solve the problem of misunderstanding. Otherwise the sons would naturally enjoy the lion's share of the parents' property after giving away their daughters in marriage.

It should be noted that one of the most basic causes for the women's inferior status is the inadequacy of the legal system to keep pace with the changing needs and times to provide her with the frame work which would enable her to contribute her ability fully to the society.

Hence, the following recommendations made by the National Committee on the status of women in India[11] should be implemented. There should be immediate reform based on broad principles like equal rights of sons and daughters and widows, and restriction on the right of testation. Adequate publicity should be given regarding the provisions available in law for women, and women are to be educated about their rights.

In the absence of social security and adequate opportunities for employment, rights of inheritance would provide financial security and save women from destitution. Even though the right to property would benefit limited section it will make women independent and help them to improve their status, effectively checking the feeling that women are a burden to the family. On divorce or separation, the wife should be entitled to the assets acquired at the time of the marriage.

Attitudes towards Social Change

The findings of Chaturvedi also show that a substantial number of respondents (75%) supported the cause of daughters for a share in parental property as a matter of asserting parity.[12]

Dowry Helps Newly Wed

Dowry was initially an institution in which gifts and presents were given to a girl at the time of her marriage when she was required to leave her parents home and join her husband's household. But unfortunately it has become a crude institution resulting in female infanticide, suicide, bride burning and other indignities and cruelties. The dowry problem has become a serious social problem among the upper castes and middle-classes in towns and villages.[13]

The growth of education, salaried employment, migration to cities and towns and scientific and industrial advancements not only increased the incidence of dowry but also changed its dimension and magnitude. Educated boys with administrative and professional jobs became the most prized prospective husbands. Those who worked in towns and cities were preferred as life was more comfortable in cities than villages. These days scooters, cars, radios, televisions, videos, refrigerators, furnitures, electrical appliances and household equipments have become a part of the dowry package among the upper sections of the society.

The respondents were asked to comment whether dowry helps in settling down the newly weds. 12.5% of them agreed and 43.75% of them disagreed while 37.5% strongly disagreed. There were 6.25% who were uncertain about the whole issue.

It could be derived from the above responses that there are some women administrators who still are unable to visualise the growing social menace. They were uncertain in deciding the whole issue and practically speaking they will not be in a position to make decisions on the problem of dowry system. The victims are not seen as instances of a particular form of oppression or of socially prevalent sex biases.

Dowry System Lowers the Status of Women

Dowry is not considered today as a gift but the right of a boy and his parents. The parents of the bridegroom spend a huge amount on their education. All this is included in the amount of dowry.

Dowry does not include cash and material goods for the bridegroom, and his parents alone, but it also includes gifts and cash for all the primary kinsmen and some other secondary and remote relatives. The groom's father exhibits the dowry to his kinsmen and fellow-beings with a sense of pride, expressing his superiority and high status.

When the respondents were asked to react to the statement, that 'dowry lowers the status of women', 62.5% of them agreed and 37.5% of them strongly agreed. It is obvious that all the respondents felt that dowry lowers the status of women. In such a condition the question arises why they are unable to solve the problem by some strict rules to check the crisis. Even though the Dowry Prohibition Act, 1961 was passed to curb the social evil of dowry which affects the dignity of women, the law remained as a paper tiger for many years, and the number of deaths of young brides continued to rise. Then the Act was amended in 1984 in response to insistent demands by the women's organisations and the words as "consideration for the marriage" have been replaced by the words, " in connection with marriage".[14]

The Dowry Prohibition (Amendment) Bill 1986 attempts to tighten the provisions of the Act and includes dowry deaths in the list of offenses in the Indian Penal Code. The Bill provides that if a woman dies within seven years of her marriage due to causes other than natural, her property would be transferred to her children and if she has no children, then to her parents. The burden of providing that no dowry demand was made, will be on those who took or abetted in the taking of the dowry, the aggrieved person will not be subjected to prosecution. This amendment bill has made the offense nonbailable and raised the minimum punishment to five years and fine up to Rs. 15,000/-. Provisions for appointment of dowry prohibition officers and their advisory board with two women members have been made.[15]

But in the existing practice of dowry system all the logical calculations lose their place and the law remains only in paper. Therefore, for the destruction of the dowry system intercaste marriages should be encouraged while arranged marriages with demands of dowry must go. There should be a new ideology inculcated in the minds of the present young generation with a value system which guarantees a place of honour to women and their parents. Young men of marriageable age should not become marketable commodities sold by their parents to the parents of brides in return for dowry.

The preventive and short-term devices should include immediate action when incidents of dowry deaths, harassment and humiliation occur. The victims of dowry should be provided legal and social protection in the true sense immediately. The television, radio and newspapers should highlight such incidents with all seriousness in order to curb the menace in future.

Casteism is a Drag on the Development and Progress

In the beginning, the caste system was started with four groups- Brahmins (Priests), Kshatriyas (Warriors), Vaisyas (Land holders and Merchants) and Sudras (Cultivators and Menials). It was a system for division of labour devised for the smooth functioning of society but later on it became a rigid system based on birth and hereditary occupation.

The British rule in India brought about diversification, differentiation and change in the caste system. In pursuance of their policy of 'divide and rule', the British encouraged continuity of the caste system. Though caste system did not remain 'organic', yet it continued to remain 'segmentary' in nature.

The respondents were asked whether casteism is a drag on the development and progress of India. About 43.75% executives agreed and 50% of them strongly agreed with the statement. But there were 6.25% of them who were uncertain of the effects of casteism. This indicates that most of the women administrators felt that casteism was a drag to the development of the social system. In several circumstances, caste acts as an interest group, a source of mobilisation at the time of elections and other occasions. The resurgence of casteism is found in many situations with new facets. The corporateness of the caste system has been eroded at the ritual level but has emerged at political and economic levels.

Intercaste Marriage Helps in National Integration

National integration is dependent upon structural, cultural and ideological congruity and harmony among different sections of a given society. Structural equality demands equal opportunity for all sections of society and more so for the depressed ones. Absence of discrimination based on caste parentage and heritage and the cultural differences are natural in Indian society because of its structural and cultural complexities, but a certain level of consensus about 'national goals' is basic for keeping people together as a nation.

With this idea the respondents were asked to comment whether the inter-caste marriages help in national integration. Almost 75% of them answered positively. Of which about 43.75% of them agreed and 31.25% of them strongly agreed, 6.25% of strongly disagreed and 18.75% of them were uncertain about it. It is clear that most of the women executives supported the intercaste marriages. It was also found that most of the respondents themselves have opted for intercaste marriages. Therefore, it should be noted that intercaste marriages can become an effective tool to solve a lot of problems relating to caste which brings divisions in the society. These findings corroborate the findings of Chaturvedi[16] and also of Girija Khanna and Marriamma Varghese.[17]

Love Marriages are More Successful

Marriage is more than a legalised sexual union between a man and women. It is socially acknowledged and approved. In India, people generally believe that marriage is not between two individuals but between two families in terms of the bonds it creates between them. Certainly marriage provides recognition of legitimacy of children. It confers acknowledged social status on the offsprings, and this is important in terms of inheritance and succession.

According to Kapadia[18] the question of selection in marriage may be considered from three points of view, namely the field of selection, the party of selection and the criteria of selection. Preferential code, prohibiting restrictions, endogamy and exogamy explain the field, the party and the criteria in the selection of marriage. Caste exercises a tremendous control over its members by imposing penalties and ostracizing on the defaulting members.

With a view to grant freedom to a person in selection of the marriage partner outside one's caste, the Special Marriage Act was passed in 1972. The Act was amended in 1923 to make it more effective. Subsequently various acts were passed in 1938, 1946 and 1949 with a view to widen the scope of selection of matters. Despite these legal enactments this freedom remains a hard fact even today.

The respondents were asked whether they considered love marriages being more successful than arranged ones because the couple get to know each other earlier. Nearly 43.75% of them felt it to be true while 18.75% of them disagreed with the statement and 37.5% of them were uncertain about it. The reasons given by those respondents who considered love marriages more successful was that it reduces the burden of dowry system. The grooms' parents cannot claim anything from the bride's parents as it is purely the boy's own choice and no option is given to the parents. Secondly, such marriages break all the taboos like the traditions and customs of the society and encourage the families to cut short unnecessary marriage expenditure. Thirdly they encourage both the families to live harmoniously without caste or creed distinctions and build the next generation without caste distinctions. Fourthly, the couples involved in marriage have a sound understanding between them and this encourages a healthy bond and atmosphere in the family. Fifthly, the couples try hard to endure all problems and tackle difficult situations to workout their marriage thus avoiding divorce.

Similarly those respondents who opposed love marriages gave their reasons that there is total opposition from either of the families and hence the couple cannot remain happy. In several families the parents disown their children and refuse to see them even till their death. Secondly, when any rift arises between the couples there is no one to treat them with love and affection. The parents, friends and relatives continuously blame their choice and try to find fault with them for making a wrong decision. Thirdly, couples may have to face the consequences all by themselves for having broken the society's norms. They may even have to forgo rights of inheritance of property in consequence of their disobedience.

From the above analysis it is clear that in spite of all the negative aspects in arranged marriages some of the respondents still supported them while majority of them were willing to break from the age old traditions and were ready to pay the cost for it. They considered love marriages suitable for the coming generations because they create a healthy and happy society. However, it should also be noted that the couples involved have to bear all the mental torture and psychological stress in order to pave way for the free healthy society. But there cannot be true happiness without any sacrifice.

Arranged Marriages are Better

In patrilineal societies, marriage signifies a transfer of a woman from her natal group to that of her husband. Arranged marriages at a young age are considered most desirable for girls, as these notions are related to the importance of virginity and the restrictions placed on marriage within the same *gotra* or clan lineage. This restriction is absent among Muslims, who prefer marriages between close relatives, as they help to keep the property within the family.

In south India cross-cousin marriages among Hindus is the accepted mode. Education and liberalisation of ideas in urban areas have led to certain changes in the patterns of selection of the marriage partners. However, some recent surveys conducted have revealed a greater preference for arranged marriages among the younger generation.[19]

Taking into consideration that the arranged marriages are better because parents are the better judges for their children, the respondents were requested to give their opinions. Varied responses to that question were found. About 12.5% of them agreed with the notion of arranged marriages and nearly 31.25% of them agreed with the idea behind it. However, majority of them (56.25%) were not sure of the entire logic. They could neither deny the fact that their parents were better judges nor could they accept blindly their parents' choice of their life partners. Their final reply was that any marriage could be a success only if the married partners were compatible and made adjustments throughout their married life.

Thus it could be concluded that no marriage could be exclusive in its own kind unless both the spouses are totally convinced with one another's view. Of course, the final decision should be given to the couple because it is their personal life and therefore the parents should not try to impose their choice on their children. However, they should explain all the pros and cons to their children and leaving them to make their own independent choice. This is explained by Promilla Kapur[20] as "neo-love marriage" and "neo-arranged marriage" where both parents and children are involved.

Nuclear Family Ensures Better Family

The nature and the characteristics of the Indian family can be traced through the ages from the Vedic to the modern period as fundamentally traditional in its nature. The Hindu home observed a joint family system which was patriarchal in nature.

In the later period there were some changes in the family life. Educated girls wanted to start independent homes. Moreover, employment opportunities were found away from the home town and therefore the nuclear family system.

The respondents were asked to highlight their views about nuclear family system. They were asked to comment on the statement – "Nuclear family helps in building a better family." Exactly 50% of them favoured the system and 50% were uncertain about the system.

It could be said from the above analysis that those who were unsure about the system were much more bothered about the negative aspects of losing the family support in bringing up their children when they devoted their time to their job.

Nuclear Family Creates Isolation and Insecurity

As the Indian culture holds closely knit family relationships, the nuclear family system appears to create isolation and feeling of insecurity in the minds of the members. They tend to lose the warmth of sharing and caring among the members of the family. The children are left alone at the mercy of servants and the entire family feels cut off from the main family because of their jobs. They cannot know the actual happenings in their family. They feel like strangers when they meet others only in some functions or occasions.

It is interesting to discover that 18.75% of the executives agreed with the negative aspects of nuclear family system, while 43.75% disagreed and 18.75% of them strongly disagreed with the statements. There were about 18.75% who could exactly support or refute the statement. Therefore, it is clear from the findings that the women executives preferred nuclear family system to the joint family system.

Widow Remarriage

There is a general strong notion that the fear of losing the relationship with their children prevents women from seeking remarriage. Social attitudes towards widows differ at different socio-economic levels, but a change in the life-style of women after widowhood is characteristic of most sections of Indian society. There seems to have been some improvement in the attitude to widows' participation in auspicious ceremonies. In spite of such marginal changes in attitude, the condition of widows continues to be a blot on our society. Therefore, the respondents were asked to react to the statement "widow should be persuaded to remarry". Interestingly enough, 31.25% of the women administrators agreed, and 25% strongly agreed while 12.5% disagreed with the statement. About 31.25% were uncertain about the view. Those respondents who disagreed with the statement felt that all widows should not be persuaded to remarry but if the widow herself decides to do so she should be able to remarry. Hence it could be said that widows should be encouraged to remarry irrespective of whether they have children or not and the society should accept this change. Even if they prefer to stay as widows the society should not restrict them from doing so while giving them the freedom to live a happy life by involving them in social and religious functions as any other individual.

Age of Marriage

The Special Marriage Act, 1954, fixes the minimum age at 21 and 18 for males and females respectively. In all the personal laws, a lower age is prescribed for girls and it is below 18 in all of them.

The Suicide Enquiry Committee appointed by the Government of Gujarat[21] reported that child marriage is one of the significant factors leading to the high incidence of suicide among young married women. Increasing the age of marriage from 18 to 21 is desirable as in the case of males because until then a girl is not physically and mentally mature for the responsibilities of parenthood.

The respondents were asked whether the minimum age of marriage for a girl should be 21 years as in the case of males. 50% of the administrators agreed and 31.25% of them strongly agreed with the statement. But surprisingly 6.25% of them disagreed and 12.5% were uncertain about the increase in age for the marriage of girls.

From the above analysis it is clear that there are women administrators who disapprove the change in the society. Educated women, take steps for a change and even influence illiterate women. Secondly, only if the girl is mature enough as the boy she can be a equal partner. Otherwise the inequalities and suppression of women would continue and there will not be any end to the violence and other abuse against women. Therefore, a change is essential for improving the standards of women in India.

Educational Qualification

Education has been regarded both as an end in itself and as a means of realising other desirable ends. It develops the personality and rationality of individuals, qualifies them to fulfill certain economic, political, and cultural functions and thereby improves their socio-economic status.

The movement for improving women's status all over the world has always emphasised education as the most significant instrument for changing women's subjugated position in society. In order to achieve this goal the respondents were to give their opinion whether the minimum educational qualification of girls should be higher secondary level. Majority of the administrators supported the view where 37.50% agreed and 31.25% strongly agreed. There were 6.25% who disagreed and 6.25% who strongly disagreed while 18.75% were not sure about the idea.

Those respondents who disapproved the statement felt that it was unthinkable for a developing country like India to enforce such a standard. However, it should be noted that only if there was something in theory, the practical part could be done. If we are not prepared for a change in theory itself then it is impossible to achieve anything in practice. We will still continue being a developing country or still go worse to an underdeveloped situation. Therefore, there is an urgency to incorporate the importance of education in the minds of people in India. Only then we could be in conformity with the rest of the world.

Importance of Women's Education

Social attitudes to girl's education vary from acceptance to absolute indifference. A detailed analysis of the attitude of women administrators towards women's education was carried. The respondents were asked to react to the following viewpoints of importance:

a. **Improves marriage prospects :** This view was accepted by 31.25% of the respondents and refuted by 18.75%, while 50% of them were uncertain.

b. **Enables to earn :** Nearly majority of the administrators felt that education helps women to become economically independent. About 50% of them agreed and 18.75% strongly agreed with the view. However, 6.25% disagreed and 25% were not sure about the issue.

c. **Helps in adverse situation :** Most of the respondents either agreed or strongly disagreed with this view. They were 56.25% and 25% respectively. Only 18.75% of them were not clear about this view.

d. **Uplifts social status :** It was interesting to know that almost all women executives felt that it is very true that education uplifts the social status of women in an Indian situation. Only 6.25% agreed and 25% strongly agreed with it.

e. **Ensures social prestige :** According to 43.75% of the respondents, this view was acceptable. 12.5% of them strongly favoured it while for 12.5% it was not untrue and for 31.25% it was an undecided thing.

Therefore, it is clear that in most of the situations education proved to be an asset for women in the Indian society.

Unemployment

Today there are unmistakably more employment opportunities for women in the modern world than ever before. On the one hand, there are women engineers, architects, managers, administrators, diplomats, politicians and ministers today. The problem of unemployment on the other hand has increased to its peak. The respondents were asked whether the unemployment increased due to the growing trend of women taking up jobs. This view was strongly accepted by 6.25% of the respondents. But was disapproved or strongly disapproved by majority of them.

Reservation of Seats for Women

As social justice is one of the prime objectives of the Indian constitution the respondents were asked to comment on the need for reservation of seats for women in education and jobs to uplift their social status. The responses were found in varied categories. While 37.5% agreed, nearly 31.25% disagreed with it and 25% of them strongly opposed the idea. Only 6.25% were uncertain about the trend.

Therefore it could be said that the executives felt that women were competent enough to compete with men and they did not require any reservation policy. It would in fact make them feel low or incompetent if there were reservations for them. There should be equality even in this case.

Exclusive Courses of Study

Co-education is an controversial area in Indian education. While arguments in its defense from the point of view of fuller utilisation of resources and economy are gradually gaining ground, it has been generally objected to by the defenders of women's education out of an apprehension that social prejudices against women's education can be removed more easily if girls are taught in separate institutions. Therefore, the women administrators were asked to give their opinion regarding exclusive courses of study for men and women. It was found that if the disparities were to be removed then, both men and women should be treated as equals right from the small age and should be allowed to mingle freely without segregation. Only then they would grow with the same mentality. Otherwise the discrimination between sexes would continue to exist.

Legalisation of Abortion

The government passed the Medical Termination of Pregnancy Act 1971 for making abortions legal. But the question arises whether this legalisation has become the root cause for the increase in premarital sex in the society leading to low moral standards. When the respondents were asked to provide their views regarding this matter, it was accepted by 12.5% and strongly supported by 6.25%. However, 43.75% of them disagreed and 18.75% of them strongly disapproved the issue. There were 18.75% who were unwilling to comment on this issue. Therefore it could be derived that according to the respondents, legalisation of abortion does have some negative impact on the Indian set up leading to increase in immorality. However, it should be borne in mind that legalisation of abortion in several nations proved to be the major cause for the breakdown of moral standards. The freedom is misused by most of the youngsters and teenagers leading to immoral traffic in school/college life. This legalisation should be applicable to genuine married couples in order to strictly avoid mental strain or physical risk for the mother.

Abortion and Termination of Unwanted Pregnancy

In most of the cases it is observed that legalisation of abortion acts as a boon for mothers or couples who want to terminate unwanted pregnancy. This helps them to kill the foetus if they do not want to continue. This in fact, affects the healthy atmosphere of accepting procreation as a gift of God. It endangers man's right in preserving a young tender life. According to the Table 4.2, 56.25% of the women executives were in favour of abortion. 18.75% disagreed with the notion, while 6.25% strongly opposed it. There were also 18.75% who stood in the intermediate position. They could not stand for or against the whole issue.

Table 4.2. Abortion and Unwanted Pregnancy

Agree	56.25%
Disagree	18.75%
Strongly disagree	6.25%
Uncertain	18.75%
Total	100.00%

Religion and Moral Life

Religion in general teaches a person to fear God and maintain the social and moral standards. Indian constitution is known for its secularism with tolerance towards all religious faiths. In the present situation of growing trend in acute problems caused due to immorality, the respondents were requested to express their views, whether religion helps in maintaining the moral life.

56.25% agreed and 31.25% strongly accepted the view respectively, while 6.25% disagreed and 6.25% strongly opposed this idea. Hence from the above analysis it is clear that majority of the respondents accepted the relationship of religion and moral life. This could be because India is basically pluralistic in religion and most of them believe in the existence of God.

Belief in God

In India it is an unquestionable fact that religion plays a vital role in every part of one's life. In fact, religion moulds the character and builds up the personality. However, to test whether education or higher position in one's life brings disbelief in God, the women administrators were asked to share their personal opinion whether belief in God reflects weak personality in a person.

Its a surprise that none agreed with the statement and most of them disagreed with it. Nearly 37.5% disagreed and 43.75% strongly disagreed with the view. About 18.75% were uncertain. It could be said that women are more religious and they believe in some faith or the other. Therefore, they could outrightly deny the existence of God in spite of being uncertain.

Belief in Fate

As science and technology have become so much advanced today, man considers himself capable of controlling most of the situations. He is at least to predict few things in advance before it could even happen. For example, the weather conditions and epidemics.

Man has a natural tendency to feel secure with the predictions and not to believe in fate. Education helps them to reason out things instead of blindly accepting fatalism. When the executives were asked to comment on whatever is bound to happen will happen, it was interesting to know that 56.25% approved fatalism and 6.25% strongly approved. While 37.5% were not sure about it. Hence, it could be derived that even though the respondents were educated women they still believed in fate.

Problem of AIDS and Immorality

Acquired Immune Deficiency Syndrome is a sexually transmitted disease from one heterogeneous couple to another. It is a shame that the latest survey proved that many of the youngsters especially teenagers were carriers of HIV positive. That means they were already diseased with AIDS and the progeny they will produce would be AIDS infected generation.

The respondents were asked whether they accepted that immoral traffic of women has increased AIDS. Most of them, about 75% agreed and 12.5% asserted strongly that it was one of the causes for increase in AIDS. About 6.25% disagreed to it and 6.25% were uncertain about the whole problem.

Even though most of the executives admitted that the problem of AIDS was due to immoral traffic of women, they were unable to stop them from doing so. Hence, the only possible solution for this problem is that the people should be educated about the consequences of AIDS and the precautions they should take.

Lower Image of Women in Media

There have been protests against media portrayal of women. In radio for instance, the songs selected depict themes of young women waiting to be married. Plays convey the message of the ideal woman who is a housewife and mother. If she is employed, then she must be neglecting her home and children. To make the programme more entertaining a woman is often portrayed as a gossip monger who cannot hold a secret and loves to go on shopping and ultimately get duped. The producers and financiers of the cinema are worried about the message of change, or content of the film. They see women as sexy, glamorous and empty headed. Over and above the traditional patriarchal values, they depict violence against women in such a stark manner that it dehumanizes the individual. Beating of wife and insults hurled at women are a part of films. The advertisement medium is very blatant and openly anti-women and treats women only as sex symbol. Advertisements show that whether a woman is used for advertising cosmetics, fabrics, jewellery or domestic gadgets or suitcases, scooters or stationery, she has to be glamorous and enticing. Even in advertisements of men's clothes is the invariable use of admiring women by the side of men which creates the impression that all a woman desires is a man dressed in sophisticated garments. TV relies considerably on commercial cinema and advertisements. Hence the stereotyped image of woman is repeated. The woman is invariably in the kitchen cooking food which is approved by her mother-in-law, washing a bucketful clothes and yet very charmingly, bandaging children's bruises and feeding her husband.

Coming to the print media, there are special women's features in the newspapers which generally depict the image of woman as a consumer and glamour-loving and confine her to the role of a wife and mother. Women's magazines particularly in English, are so casual in their approach to the problems of women that one wonders whether there is any serious message regarding women's status or problems.

The women administrators were asked whether the degrading image of women in the media and magazines reduces the status of women. 43.75% of them agreed with the view and 50% of them strongly agreed with the statement. But 6.25% of the respondents were not sure on this issue. It could therefore be said that the executives themselves were unaware of the sensitive degrading status of women and even if they were aware they could practically do nothing about it because they felt that the deal was between the media industry and the financiers which is a profit-oriented business. Cinema is the cheapest means of entertainment in a poor country like India. They cannot check the financiers and producers or directors at every level. They can only regulate the licenses and release of films through the censor board. However, it is clear that something should be done to educate the public in a better manner to improve the status of women. The directors should be taught to better the image of women and produce good quality films. There should be a committee representing the general public, women organisation, journalists, representatives both from the government and media to analyse and evaluate the programmes and items published in order to improve the quality of entertainment.

Prostitution to be Legalised

The commercialisation of this old profession is a recent phenomenon. It is believed that the entrants to this profession are victims of social oppression and poverty. In the absence of adequate employment opportunities, families in poorer and even the middle-classes are compelled to encourage prostitution. Wives of bonded and other agricultural labourers take up this occupation to free their families from indebtedness. In some areas girls are encouraged to earn their dowries. This is only the exploitation of the poor by the rich and of women by men.

The respondents were asked whether prostitution should be legalised. According to 12.5% of them this profession helps the poor to earn a living and secondly if it is legalised the negative effects like increase in sexually transmitted diseases could be avoided by regular check ups and use of contraceptive methods. However, 31.25% of them disagreed and 37.5% strongly disagreed and considered prostitution as a form of exploitation of women and felt that the victims should be sent to rehabilitation centres and the profession should be banned. However, nearly 18.75% of the respondents did not express their views. They were certain about the whole issue.

Sex Test

Various techniques of sex determination and sex preselection have been discovered, foetoscopy, needling, chorion bioscopy and amniocentesis are increasingly becoming household names in

India. Although these techniques were supposed to be used mainly to detect genetic deformities, in India they are used for the detection of the sex of foetus and thereafter extermination of female foetus through abortion. Between 1978 and 1983 around 78,000 female foetuses were aborted after sex determination tests in the country.[22]

The women administrators were asked whether sex tests endangers women's right. Around 37.5% of the women executives agreed with the statement, 6.25% of them strongly believed it, while 31.25% of them disagreed because it did not affect their rights. They could make use of the available technology and 25% were uncertain about the issue. It could be said that most of the women executives do not seem to realise the present crisis women are facing. If they encourage sex tests, implications of the test must be highlighted to the public through media coverage and various other methods like posters, campaigns, exhibitions, condemning the tests.

Status of Women

Women's struggle have challenged the existing system which has made them socially, culturally, economically and even politically, crippled. The respondents were asked to express their views regarding elevation of the status of women.

   a. *By Economic Independency* : 56.25% of the respondents agreed and 31.25% of them strongly supported this view and 12.5% were not sure whether economic independency really elevated the status of women.

   b. *By Active Participation in Politics* : According to 3.25% of the respondents the status of women is elevated when they actively take part in politics. But 25% of them refuted this statement. About 43.75% of the executives were not clear about the problem. Therefore, it could be said that for most of them active participation of women in politics need not necessarily uplift the status of women.

   c. *By Recognition of their Authority in Domestic Life* : The identity of a woman is generally defined by her role within the family. If she expresses herself as an independent individual or a person she is put to a lot of hardship. The women executives were asked to comment on the statement that the status of women is elevated by recognition of their authority in domestic life. The majority of the executives supported the statement. To 75% of them this view was acceptable and to 6.25% it was strongly acceptable, while 18.75% were not sure. Hence from the above view point of the respondents it could be derived that majority of the women executives agreed with the elevation of the status of women by economic independency and their authority in domestic life. However, the participation of women in politics did not necessarily improve their status. It should be noted that it is not merely the achievement or position which is needed. The basic recognition of women as a person and an individual in the family and society alone helps in the upliftment of the status of women.

Neutralisation of the Constitutional Rights

Women are lagging behind men in several areas because of India's social and cultural heritage and strong tradition of patriarch and male domination. Even though several legislations have been passed by the Government of India regarding marriage, inheritance of property, divorce, dowry, rate etc., in addition to what was incorporated in the constitution regarding equality and against discrimination based on religion, race, caste and sex. These social legislations have not been very effective in India.

The women administrators were asked to comment on the statement that continuing trends of social inequality have neutralised constitutional and legal provisions of equality. 43.75% of them accepted the statement to be true and 31.25% believed that it is very much true. However, 6.25% of them could not accept this view point, while 18.75% of the executives were uncertain about the situation.

Basically the problem is due to unequal access of men and women to society's resources and its distributive processes. Therefore, women are to be educated about the constitutional and legal remedies available to them. They should come forward boldly, shedding their fear and make use of the opportunities. The victims should also be supported and encouraged by other women and men of the society to avail themselves of the privileges conferred on them by legislations.

Conclusion

From the above study it could be said that the attitude of women administrators towards social changes like equality of men and women and equality in the inheritance of property was accepted by majority of them. They differed in their views on the dowry system. Some of them considered that dowry helps the newly wed. However, surprisingly all of them felt that dowry lowers the status of women. What is considered to be given as a gift to help the couples should not be demanded and become an evil practice. Almost all the respondents considered casteism as a drag on development. The solution to this problem was to encourage intercaste marriage which would help promote national integration.

The reactions to love marriages, arranged marriages, nuclear family system and widow remarriage were complex. Equalising the age of marriage for girls as 21 years with boys was supported by majority of them. Similarly, the increase in the minimum qualification of girls to higher secondary was supported by most of them, while few of them felt that it was not possible in a situation like India.

In most of the situations, education proved to be an asset for women. For majority of the respondents problem of unemployment was not due to increase in women taking up jobs.

Reservation policy for women was not supported by all of them. They felt that they were competent enough to fight with men. It is believed by all respondents that coeducation helps to bridge the gap between the sexes.

Legalisation of abortion was a controversial subject. Majority of the respondents did relate religion and morality. None of the women administrators accepted that belief in God reflects weak personality. They also believed in fatalism. Though the executives could relate the problem of AIDS to immorality, they felt that they could not stop it. The degrading image of women in media was opposed by majority of the respondents but they felt that they could do nothing about it. Legalisation of prostitution was opposed by the executives. Sex test determination was not accepted as a threat by all the administrators. Some felt they could make use of the available technology.

The idea whether economic independency of women really elevated the status of women was questionable. The general view point of women administrators was that active participation in politics by women does not necessarily uplift the status of women. For majority of the respondents recognition of the authority of women in domestic life elevated the status of women.

For most of the women administrators the continuing trends of social inequality of men and women in India have neutralised the constitutional and legal rights. According to William J Goode, "we must never underestimate the cunning or the staying power of those in chare".[23] Therefore, if the women administrators make use of their powers, they can do a lot more to uplift the status of women in India.

Family in India has been explained as purely functional or a distinctive cultural feature of the subcontinent. Social scientists have been engaged in debate on the topics like "nuclearisation of joint family structure is taking place in India" and "nuclearisation of joint family structure is not taking place".[24] Nevertheless, it would be simplistic to say that we are on the brink of profound change in the social structure in the direction of equality and justice.

Notes and References

[1] Devasundaram, Suguna "Roots of Suppression of Women in India", C.S.I. Women's Fellowship, Bangalore, 1992, p. 51.
[2] Sinha, Niraj, *Women and Violence*, New Delhi: Vikas Publishing House Pvt. Ltd, 1989.
[3] *Indian Express*, Editorial, 27 April, 1984.
[4] Kelkar, Govind, "Violence against Women: An Understanding of Responsibility for Their Lives", *Samya Shaki* 2, no.1, (1985): 56-57.
[5] Sharma, K.L., *Indian Society*, New Delhi, NCERT, 1990, p 180.
[6] Mehta, Vimla, *Attitude of Educated Women Towards Social Issues*, New Delhi: National Publishing House, 1979, p.1.
[7] Ray, N.K., *Women's Role in National Development*, Documentation on Women's concerns, Library and Documentation Centre, All India Association For Higher Education, October to December, New Delhi, 1991, p. 71.

[8] Desai, Neera and Maithreyi Krishnaraj, *Women and Society in India*, Delhi: Ajantha Publications, 1987, pp. 317-318.
[9] Sayeed, Badar, "Property Rights and Women" Paper unpublished by Penn, Centre of Women's Studies, Mylapore, Madras, p. 10.
[10] "Status of Women in India", *ICSSR*, New Delhi, p. 55.
[11] Ibid, p. 55.
[12] Chaturvedi, Geeta, *Women Administrators of India*, Jaipur: RBSA Publications, 1985, p. 563.
[13] Sharma, K.L., *Indian Society*, New Delhi: NCERT, 1990, p. 133.
[14] Desai, and Maithreyi, Op. cit., p. 314.
[15] Ghadially, Rehana, *Women in Indian Society*, New Delhi: Sage Publications, 1988, p. 177.
[16] Chaturvedi Op. cit., p.57.
[17] Khanna, Girija and A. Varghese Mariamma, *Indian Women Today*, New Delhi: Vikas Publications, 1978, p. 112.
[18] Kapadia, K.M., *Marriage and Family in India*, Calcutta: Oxford University Press, 1964.
[19] Report of the National Committee, *ICSSR*, p. 21.
[20] Kapur, Promilla, *Love, Marriage and Sex*, New Delhi: Vikas Publications, 1974, p. 82.
[21] Report of the Suicide Enquiry (Pushpaberi) Committee, Government of Gujarat, 1964.
[22] Patel, Vibhuti, "Sex Determination and Sex Preselection Tests : Abuse of Advanced Technologies", Ed. by Rehana Ghadially, *Women in Indian Society*, New Delhi: Sage Publications, 1985, p. 178-181.
[23] Goode, William J., *"Why Men Resist" in rethinking the family, some feminist questions*, Ed, by Barrie Thorne and Marilyn Yalom, Orient Longman, 1982, p. 132.
[24] Narain, Dhirendra ed; *Explorations in the Family and Other Essays*, Bombay: Thacker & Co, 1975. See Chapters I and II, Also see M.G. Kulkarni, "Family Research in India", in P.K.B. Nayar, ed., *Sociology in India; Retrospect and Prospect,* Delhi: B.R. Publishing Corporation, 1982.

5

Opinion about Political System

Introduction

In the recent years the term Political System is being preferred by political scientists over the earlier terms Government, State, or Nation. However, it is not merely a change in nomenclature but much more. The term political system includes certain processes and activities which were not formerly considered a part of political mechanism, and hence is more comprehensive. In the 1930's and 1940's, there was an uneasy alliance between feminism and nationalism.[1] While women organisations accepted a subordinate and complementary role in politics they repeatedly came in conflict with the Congress when it threatened women's issues and alienated women members from the Dandi March in 1930. The Women's Indian Association protested and demanded that "no demonstration organised for the welfare of India should prohibit women from a share in them"[2].

General Feature of Political System

The political system has some characteristics which are as follows:

1. Firstly, it differs from other systems. It has an exclusive power to use legitimate force. In other words, it has the right to use force and command obedience with the help of force.

2. Secondly, political system includes apart from the formal governmental institutions i.e., legislature, executive and judiciary, other traditional structures like kinship, ties, caste groupings and other phenomena like associations,

riots, demonstrations and formal organisations like parties and pressure groups.

3. Thirdly, the various parts of the system are interdependent and some kind of boundary exists between the system and the environments. As a result of interdependence, changes in one part leads to changes in the whole system. Further, the working of the system is greatly affected by the domestic and foreign environments.

4. Fourthly, the political system is quite comprehensive in the sense that it includes all interactions between formal and informal institutions.

5. Fifthly, the political system being a part of the social system, performs various roles. The individuals who have a role in the political system also perform their roles in other social systems and naturally there are frequent shifts in the boundary of the political system. Thus the boundaries of the political system are greatly extended during the times of election as well as during war conditions.[3]

As we turn to the specific context of India, we find that the evolution of political institutions, norms and processes are neither nor entirely contributions of tradition. On the contrary, the colonial antecedents of the immediate past cumulatively present the legacy and the core of what could be identified as indices of political modernisation.[4]

Inevitably, federal-parliamentary democratic political system based on socio-economic justice, secularism, educational, agrarian and industrial productivity, mixed economy and planning and decentralised democracy were introduced as vital bases of political modernisation.[5]

The assumption in the present study is that educated women including, working women, might or might not support active participation in the political process, but they certainly are adequately informed as much as they are conscious as citizens of a democratic political system.

Women administrators were asked to react to specific questions bearing upon some major dimensions of the political process in India. Their opinion was sought in order to find out their understanding about the political system which is suitable for the effective functioning of India.

Democratic System is Best

Democracy is the rule by the people. It is the will of the people. Men and women decide as to who should rule and what are the goals. The respondents of the study were asked to comment on the statement – "Democratic system of government is the best form of government for India". Majority of the respondents supported the statement. About 68.75% agreed and 18.75% of them strongly agreed with it, while 12.5% were uncertain about the suitability of the system. However, the question arises as to who participates in political decisions, which is one of the most fundamental question of democracy.

Democratic System is Unsuitable

Similarly, the respondents were asked to present their view on the statement – "Democratic system is unsuitable to India" because there is a notion that India needs a totalitarian regime at least for a few years in order to eradicate corruption and unhealthy practices in the government. The responses make clear that a small percentage of 6.25% agreed with the view while most of them disagreed. Nearly 56.25% opposed the idea and 31.25% of them strongly opposed the notion. There were 6.25% who again were not sure of the situation. Therefore, it is clear from the views above that democracy is the best system of government for India but the participation of the people needs to be improved in order to make it more effective.

Proportional Representation is Best

In a true democracy every section should be adequately represented. Proportional representation is an electoral device that seeks to create a representative body that reflects the distribution of opinion in the electorate. Where majority or plurality systems effectively reward strong parties and penalise the weak one by assigning authority to represent the whole constituency to a candidate who may have received half or less of the votes.

Opinion about Political System

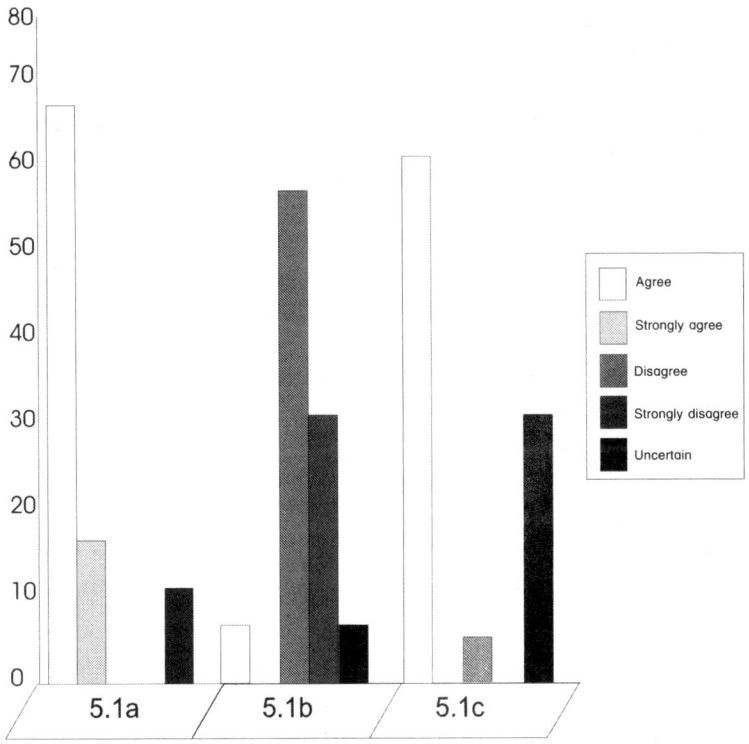

Fig. 5.1. Administrators' response towards different statement.

5.1a. Democratic system is best
5.1b. Democratic system is unsuitable
5.1c. Proportional representation is best.

Proportional representation ensures minority groups a measure of representation proportional to their number.[6] From fig 5.1(c) it is clear that 62.5% of the women administrators favoured the system and 6.25% felt it to be unsuitable while 31.25% of them were not sure about the working of it. It could be said that although in theory proportional representation has everything in its favour but in practice it is not effective because no single political party is able to capture clear cut majority. Coalition governments are the inevitable result and they fall whenever one section or group of the coalition withdraws its support. Secondly it gives rise to minority thinking while formulating polities and programmes contributing to successful sectionalism.

Universal Adult Franchise

The term universal adult franchise" means a system where all the adult nationals of a country except certain categories of persons like minors, criminals, lunatics are entitled to become voters and participate in the elections without any distinction of caste, colour, creed, profession, sex and status.

The respondents were asked whether the principle of universal adult franchise ensures equality and establishes true democracy. Fig 5.2(a) shows the responses which are as follows. 56.25% of the respondents approved and 6.25% strongly approved the system while 6.25% disapproved it and 31.25% were uncertain about the effects.

Even though the system ensures equality and establishes true democracy it also suffers from certain serious shortcomings and is fraught with many dangers, the chief argument being that it is unsuitable for illiterate masses who may misuse it.

Two Party System is Necessary in India

The merit of the two party system is that it ensures stable government as compared to the multiparty system. This stability is the result of the fact that all the ministers in the ministry are taken from one party and not from many irreconcilable groups or factions. Therefore, this homogeneity helps them to work as a team under their leader, the prime minister. In a cabinet type of government, the prime minister can count on the loyalty of his colleagues as will as the majority in the parliament and pursue policies in a systematic manner.

Another important advantage of this system is that it secures a truly representative government. In such a system, both the parties have well-defined programmes and a direct appeal is made to the voters on the basis of these programmes. The voters are in a

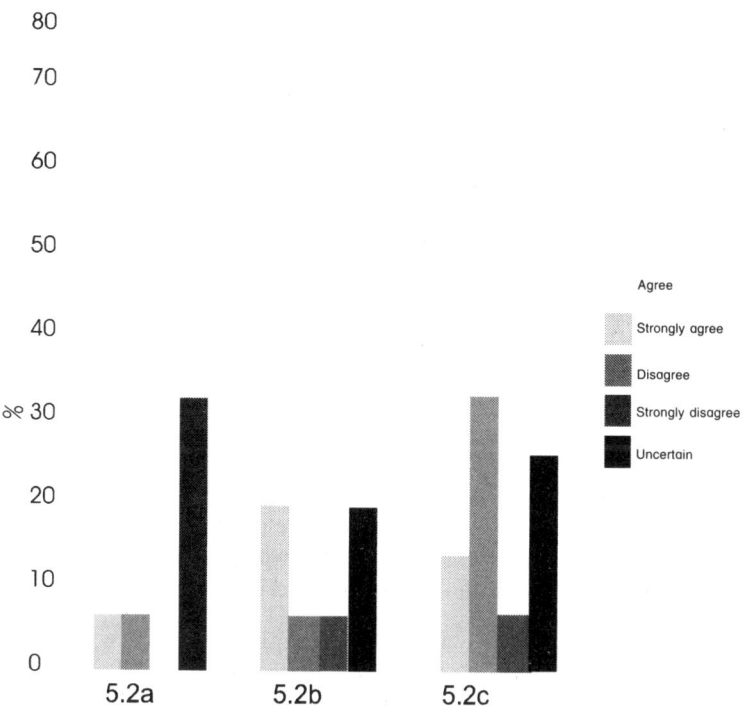

Fig. 5.2. Administrators' response towards different statements

5.2a. Universal adult franchise
5.2b. Two party system is necessary in India
5.2c. Socialism is compatible with democracy

position to decide clearly about the party which they want. They have two alternatives. One of the two parties will win a majority and become responsible for the enactment of policies, the other will form the opposition both having a well-organised and disciplined following with clearly defined policies.[7]

The women executives were asked whether two strong political parties are necessary for the success of parliamentary democracy in India. Fig 5.2(b) is self-explanatory showing that 50% of the executives approved the statement and 18.75% strongly agreed with it. However, 6.25% disagreed and 6.25% strongly disapproved the idea. About 18.75% were uncertain about the suggestion. The negative view point was that it leads to dictatorship of one party which tends to become undemocratic.

Socialism is Incompatible with Democracy

Dating back to the national movement in India, socialism and democracy have been looked as viable instruments for the achievement of the goals of a just and equitable socio-economic and political order. The spirit of that faith could be identified in the Constitution of India.[8]

On the other hand Singhi's study concluded that a large number of bureaucrats consider democracy and socialism inadequate instruments for national development.[9] It is also stated that democracy and socialism are incompatible and any attempt to synthesise the two value systems could be counter productive.[10]

The respondents were asked to give their views on the statement – Socialism is incompatible with democracy. In response to this statement about 25% of them agreed and 12.5% of them strongly refuted the idea. There were 25% of them who did not want to comment on the statement. This is evident in Fig 5.2(c).

It could be seen from the above responses that there was difference of opinion in each category. There seems to be an equal decision.

Judicial System in India

The judiciary acts as the interpreter and guardian of the constitution. The judiciary can declare a law as unconstitutional if it is convinced that the rights, privileges or immunity guaranteed by the constitution are being denied to the citizens. This power of the judiciary is termed as 'power of judicial review'.

The actual working of the judicial review all these years has demonstrated that the doctrine has failed to strike a happy compromise between the two extremes of legislature impatience for social reform and the judicial insistence on constitutional protection of individual rights. In short, the judicial review in India has failed to keep pace with the march of time[11].

The respondents were asked to comment on the statement that 'India's judicial system is time-consuming and complicated'. Overwhelming majority of the executives declared that it is very true. About 43.75% agreed and the same percentage of respondents strongly believed the statement to be true. There were 12.5% of them who were not able to comment on the statement. It could be seen in fig 5.3(a) clearly that majority of them considered the judiciary in India to be a failure. However, it should be noted that even if the courts have failed to march with time the remedy does not lie in doing away with judicial review. Better results can be achieved by associating persons having knowledge of social sciences and administrative processes with the judiciary. The doctrine of 'popular sovereignty' can be given greater importance by vesting in legislature the power to overrule or reserve the decisions of the courts by a two-third majority. These suggestions will certainly go a long way in eliminating the evils of judicial review[12].

Promotions of Civil Servants

The efficiency of civil services also depends on reasonable chances for promotion to higher posts. Promotions are a sort of reward for meritorious and faithful services. Promotion can be made either on the basis of seniority or merit. The women executives were asked whether the promotion of the civil servants should be granted strictly on the basis of merit.

The response in Fig 5.3(b) shows that 43.75% approved and 12.5% strongly approved the statement while 25% disapproved it. Nearly 18.75% were not willing to comment. It should be noted that the best system of promotion tries to combine the principle of seniority and merit together.

Representation in Civil Services

If the efficiency of the civil services is to be maintained it is desirable that the civil services must be completely integrated in the community, in keeping with the spirit of democracy. The question was put before the respondents whether the civil service

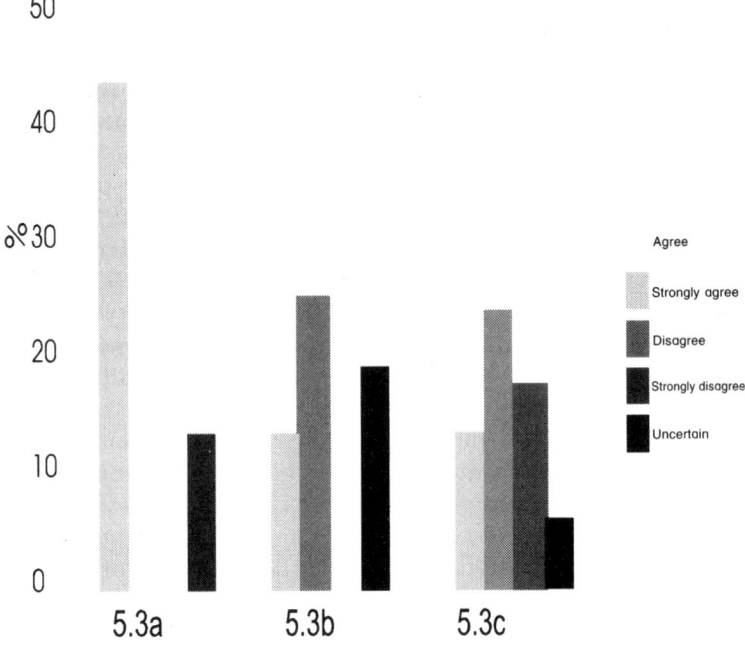

Fig. 5.3. Administrators' response towards different statements

5.3a. India's judicial system is time-consuming
5.3b. Promotion of civil servants should be based on merit
5.3c. Civil services should be represented by various socio-economic classes.

should be represented by the various social and economic classes in the community.

From Fig 5.3(c) it is clear that 37.5% agreed and 12.5% strongly agreed with the statement, while 25% disregard and 18.75% strongly disagreed respectively. About 6.25% were uncertain about the idea. In the past the higher civil services were drawn predominantly from a privileged minority. In recruiting members of the civil service and promoting men to higher positions emphasis should be laid on the administrative ability and high intellectual capacity of the candidates. The services should not be permitted to be dominated by any one favoured group. Then the civil services will become highly competent, responsive and responsible.

Recruitment in Civil Services

The first factor essential for raising a body of efficient civil services is the rational method of recruitment of civil servants on the basis of merit rather than favouritism. This can be achieved through an open competition for recruitment which was first evolved in Great Britain.

However, for the benefit of the oppressed and underprivileged sections where the opportunities are meagre the respondents were asked whether they should have any relaxation especially for the underprivileged or they should compete in open competition.

Surprisingly, it is clear in Fig 5.4(a) that almost all of them supported the statement that recruitment in civil services should be based on merit. 50% of them agreed and 43.75% strongly approved. Only 6.25% were not sure.

Alottment of Specific Tasks

As the civil servants are practically connected with everything done in their official capacity and are termed as 'statesmen in disguise' the office procedures must be quick. Civil servants must not behave as slaves of rules and regulations and must consider all cases on merit. They must take independent decisions and not shirk responsibility. In order to get better results the respondents were questioned whether they should be allotted specific tasks to complete instead of jurisdiction.

In response to this statement the women executives seemed to be unhappy about the suggestion where about 12.5% of them agreed and 6.25% strongly disagreed to it while 37.5% did not want to give their views. This is shown in fig 5.4(b). Therefore it could be said that if allotment of specific tasks was given to civil servants instead of jurisdiction that would not help them to complete their work happily.

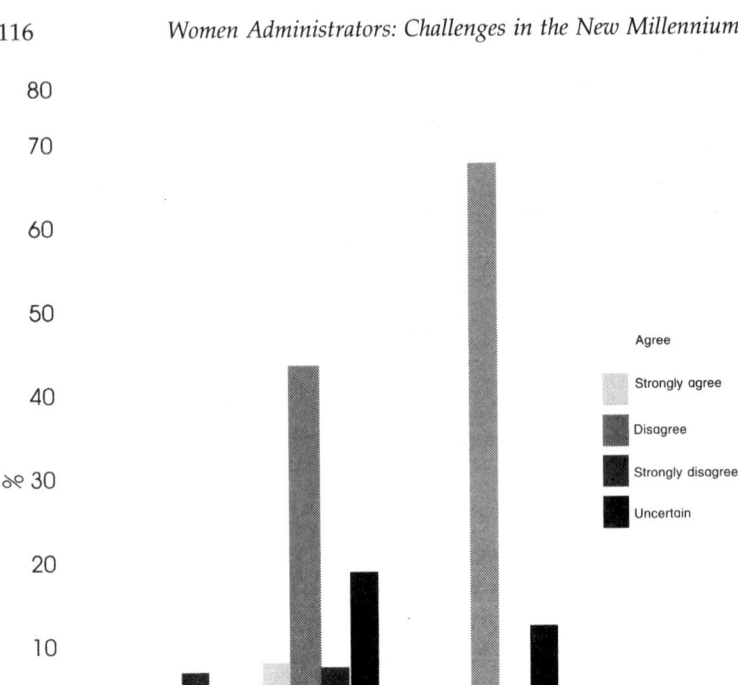

Fig. 5.4. Administrators' response towards different statements

5.4a. Recruitment in civil service should be on merit
5.4b. Civil servants should be alloted specific tasks
5.4c. Civil servants should have the right to strike

Right to Strike

The question whether the civil servants should be given the right to strike or not is a very controversial one and divergent views have been expressed on this issue.

The women administrators were asked whether civil servants should have the right to go on strike. It could be seen from Fig 5.4(c) that only 12.5% of the respondents agreed with the view while majority of them 68.75% disagreed and 6.25% strongly disapproved the idea of going on strike. About 12.5% were not sure of the trend.

Hence it could be seen that the respondents themselves felt it was not proper for them as representatives of the government to go on strike. They should be able to set an example to the employees of private enterprises for smooth functioning without causing inconvenience to the general public.

Women are Unsuitable for Politics

In the present Indian society women have obtained social economic rights and are trying to play a positive role in the development of society. They have also proved that they are no less than their counterparts by making their presence felt in most professions. But in politics, they are found to be far behind their male colleagues. Woman have not made much impact on Indian politics today. Their role in politics has not been accepted in the same way as that of men. The poor participation of women is perhaps an indication of their disillusionment with the unhealthy trends in politics like corruption and inefficiency in all spheres of political activity. It can also be because of the tender, graceful and soft spoken nature of women which is unsuited to the rough Indian politics.[13]

The respondents were asked to comment on the statement "women should not contest elections because they are physically weaker than men and are incapable of discharging the duties of citizenship". It is clear from Fig 5.5(a) that only 6.25% of the respondents strongly agreed to the analysis, while 25% disagreed and 68.75% strongly disapproved the notion. This is seen even in Dr. Chaturvedi's study where women executives who expressed the view that women should contest elections.[14] Besides voting which is accepted almost without exception as the standard political act, there are three other modes of political participation: campaign activity, cooperative activity and citizen initiated contacts.[15]

Reservation of Seats in Parliament

Many factors are important in the election of women candidates such as literacy, family background, family financial position, involvement in politics, local candidates, campaign strategy, pull within the party and personality. The combined result of all these factors is that very few women are given party tickets or can fight elections as independent members and out of them naturally even fewer can get seats in the legislature.[16]

As the political participation of women in India is meagre the respondents were asked whether there should be reservation of seats for women in Parliament and state legislatures in order to encourage them to enter politics.

In response to this question, Fig 5.5(b) shows clearly that the views of the women administrators differed altogether. About 43.75% supported the statement and 12.5% strongly agreed, while 12.5% disagreed and nearly 25% strongly refuted the idea. There were 6.25% who were uncertain about the issue. Even though there was a demand for reservation of seats for women earlier it was rejected after examination with a majority decision dissenting in the national committee.[17]

Therefore, it could be said from the above analysis that women in India should clamour for reservation of seats in legislatures as they showed clamour for their concern with problems like price rise, unemployment, poverty, dowry deaths that affected their day-to-day lives. Only then they can prove that they are really interested in political participation. Political participation means active involvement of the people in the decision-making activity of the government.[18]

Freedom of Mass media

Mass media are specifically specialised and differentiated structures conducive to purposive communication and transmission of information. It is expected that freedom of the press and the level and extent of autonomy of communication structures should not be adversely controlled or restrained. Freedom of the mass media is integrally linked to the maintenance of free government.[19]

Opinion about Political System

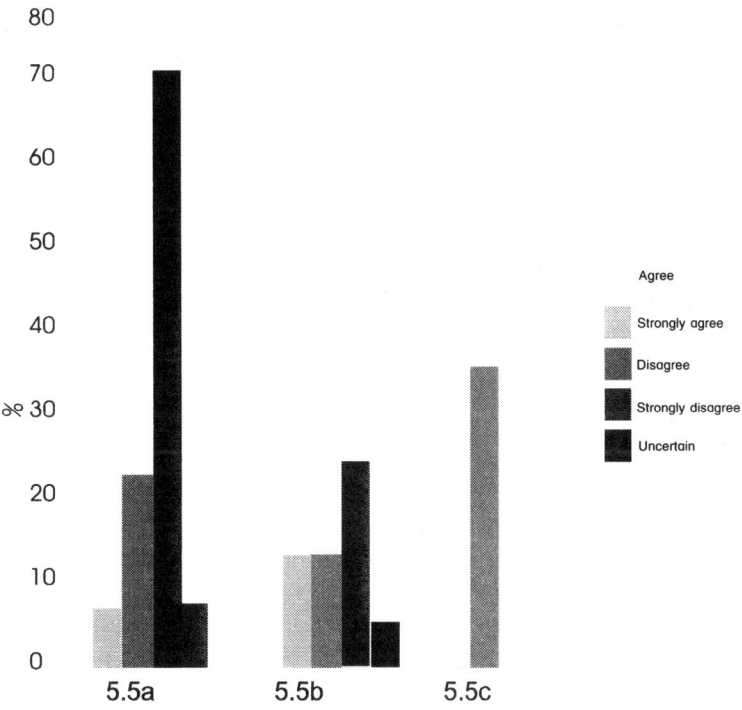

Fig. 5.5. Administrators' response towards different statements

5.5a. Women should not contest elections
5.5b. Reservation of seats for women in parliament
5.5c. Freedom of mass media is essential in democracy

Respondents were asked whether freedom of the press and the autonomy of radio and television are necessary instruments for healthy growth of democracy in India. It is obvious from Fig 5.5(c) that all the women administrators unanimously supported the statement. About 62.5% agreed and 37.5% strongly agreed with it. It is a surprise that all the respondents without any exception agreed that freedom of mass media is essential in a democracy.

This confirms that a free press has the potential to check and regulates the performance of all political functions.[20]

Conclusion

The opinion of women administrators about political system in India reflects the view that democracy is best for India but the participation of the people needs to be improved.

A great number of them felt that proportional representation is necessary for representation of minorities and universal adult franchise should be followed to establish true democracy.

The respondents differed in their opinion about the idea of having two strong parties in India. Similarly, there was difference of opinion among the respondents on socialism and its relevance in democracy.

Majority of the administrators agreed that the judiciary in India is a failure. Regarding promotions of civil servants some felt that it should be strictly based on merit, while some of them did not share this view. Nearly 50% of the respondents agreed and the other 50% disagreed that representation in civil services should be from various social and economic classes in the community.

Almost all the respondents supported that recruitment in civil services should be based on merit.

The idea of allotment of specific tasks instead of jurisdiction to civil servants was not welcomed by most of them. Majority of the respondents did not approve the right of civil servants to go on strike. Most of them disagreed with the view that women are unsuitable for politics.

Reservation of seats in legislature for women was supported by some and disapproved by some. However, freedom of mass media was accepted by all the respondents without any exception as they felt it was essential for the healthy growth of democracy in India.

Women were urged to participate in the struggle for freedom of the country. Gandhiji viewed women's oppression nearly universal. He lamented their non-participation in social, political affairs and their sexual subjection.[21]

In Gandhi's views, the qualities of courage, endurance and moral strength made women the 'natural leaders' of a non-violent struggle against unjust socio-political system. He wanted to 'feminise politics' because women had the potential to give a blow to the established socio-political power structure and could be vanguards of a non-violent struggle for a just and non-exploitative socio-political order.[22] Gandhi also said that women supplement the meagre resource of the family, but man remains the bread winner. She is essentially the mistress of the house. If he is the bread winner, she is the keeper and distributor of the bread.[23]

Notes and References

[1] Forbes, Geraldine, "The Indian Women's Movement: Struggle for Women's Right or National Liberation in the Extended Family", *Women and Political Participation in India and Pakistan*, ed., Gail Minault, Delhi: Chanakya Publications, 1981.

[2] Sharma, R.K., *Nationalism, Social Reform and Indian Women*, New Delhi: Janaki Prakashan, 1981, p.65.

[3] Srivastava, L.N., *Comparative Political Systems – Theory and Practice of Modern Government*, Fourth Revised Edition, Delhi: SBD Enterprises, 1988, pp.10-14.

[4] Nettle, J.P,.and R. Roland, *International System and the Modernisation of Societies*, Faber & Faber, 1968, pp. 45-46.

[5] Kothari, Rajini (ed) *Caste in Indian Politics*, New Delhi: Orient Longman, 1970, M.N.Srinivas, *Caste in Modern India and Other Essays*, Bombay, 1964; M.Weiner, *Politics of Society*, Chicago: University of Chicago Press, 1962; A. Beteille, *Caste Class and Power*, Bombay: Oxford University Press, 1967; and L.I. Rudolph and S.H. Rudolph, *The Modernity of Indian Tradition: Political Development in India*, New Delhi: Orient Longman, 1969, Chandler Morse et al., (ed.), *Modernisation by Design*, Calcutta: Scientific Book Agency, 1972.

[6] *The New Encyclopedia Britannica*, 15th Edition, Volume 9, p.732.

[7] Srivastava Op.cit., pp.387-390.

[8] Park, R.C., and B. Bueno de Mesquita, *India's Political System*, New Jersey: Prentice Hall, 1979, p.40.

[9] Singhi, N.K., *Bureaucracy: Positions and Persons*, New Delhi: Abhinav Publishing House, 1974, p.290.

[10] Ibid., p.171.

[11] Srivastava, Op.cit., p.269-282.

[12] Ibid., p.288.

[13] Jolly, Sushma, "Women: Too Soft for Politics", *Femina*, July 1982.

[14] Chaturvedi, *Women Administrators of India*, Jaipur: RBSA Publishers, 1985, p.116.

[15] Verba, Sydney, Bashiruddin Ahmed and Anil Bhatt, *Caste, Race & Politics*, Beverly Hills: Sage Publications, 1971, p.29.

[16] Desai, Neera and Maithreiji Krishnaraj, *Women and Society in India*, Delhi: Ajanta Publications, 1987, p.304.
[17] Report of the National Committee on "Status of Women in India", *ICSSR*, New Delhi, p.115.
[18] Almond and G.B. Powell (Jr), *Comparative Politics: A Development Approach*, New Delhi: Amerind Publishing Company Pvt. Ltd., 1972, pp.169-171.
[19] Pandey, Sumana, *Women in Politics*, Jaipur: Rawat Publications, 1990, p.12.
[20] Ibid., p.170
[21] Mazumdar, Vina, "Another Development with Women: A View from Asia" In *Development Dialogue*, the Dag Hammerskjold Foundation, Uppsala, 1982, pp.1-2 & 67-68.
[22] Dasgupta, Sugata, "Emancipation of Women in India", unpublished paper prepared for the committee on the status of women in India.
[23] Gandhi, M.K., *Women and Social Injustice*, Ahmedabad: Navjivan Publishing House, 1947, p.27.

6

Perspective on Economic Development

Introduction

The concept of development refers to a change in the desired direction. Y. Singh[1] refers to development as a strategy of planned social change in a direction which is considered desirable by the members of a society. According to him, "The notion of development may differ from society to society based on its socio-cultural background and political and geographical situation". Thus, development is a value-loaded concept, specific to the socio-cultural and economic needs of a given society, region and people.

Gunnar Myrdal[2] in his study, *Asian Drama* observes that the quest for rationality is the basis for development in the economic and social fields. Development can be brought about through planning, which is a rationally co-ordinate system of policy measures.

In general, India will come under the category of poverty stricken nation, since 45% of its population lives below the poverty line. Huts, slums and pavement dwellers give a cultural shock to visitors who come from abroad specially from developed countries. Though nearly half a country has passed since India became an independent country, the poverty has still not left its shores. It is a pain to all concerned.

In the post independent period, the government struggled to implement land ceiling which has been fully implemented. The out-castes and the poors have lived so long in the degrading situation, that they are almost settled in pauperism. The Indian society takes it as the life-style of India. There are several anomalies and contradictions in the professed policies and their implementation.

In this context, the women administrators were to comment on the economic system which will be suitable for the Indian society.

Mixed Economy

The emphasis on mixed economy emanated from the realisation that democratic socialism strengthened by the right of the citizens to elect a representative government was a viable systemic ideology. It was assumed that the government would come forward to take initiative in nation-building and the masses would be enthused to play an active role in the developmental programmes.[3]

Likewise, for the creation of socialistic pattern of society, it was necessary that both state capitalism and private monopoly, were effectively managed and controlled to avoid concentration of economic power in either of the two sectors. The operational dimension of mixed economy thus entrusts the developmental responsibilities to the public as well as the private sector. Intervention by political parties and trade unions at times becomes a bottleneck.

The respondents of this study were asked to comment on the statement "Mixed economy is unsuitable to a country like India" Around 6.25% of the respondents agreed with the statement. While majority of the respondents about 68.75% disagreed and 12.5% strongly disagreed with it, about 12.5% were uncertain about the situation.

Progressive Tax System

The respondents were asked about a progressive tax system imposing relatively heavier tax burdens on the rich and a pattern of expenditure which would confer larger benefits on the poor is ideal for India 62.5% of the executives supported the system of progressive taxation and 18.75% of them strongly agreed with the view. However, 6.25% of them were unhappy about the idea and 12.5% were not sure about the working of the system.

Fiscal Federalism

The Indian Constitution is federal in form, though the word 'federalism' has now here been used in the constitution. The constitution describes it as a 'Union of States'. The framers of the Indian Constitution were of the opinion that the country could not be efficiently governed as a unitary state. For a big country like India having vast territory, great diversity of race, religion and language, it was essential to have a federal unity.

Unlike the US Federation, the Indian Federation is not the result of agreement by the units. Secondly, the federating units have no independence for complete autonomy. The Indian Constitution follows the Canadian model.[4]

However, in recent days certain disquieting features have been seen in the Indian federation. Many federating units or the states have political parties of different complexion in power other than party in power at the centre. This has resulted in the conflict between the centre and the states. The conflict is with regard to many factors, the most important being in the economic sphere. The states accuse the federal government of economic domination and demand a free hand in the distribution of funds.

In this context, the women executives were asked to state whether "In India there is a serious need for a radical restructuring of fiscal federalism in favour of the states."

About 68.75% of them favoured the view and 12.5% strongly supported the idea, while 12.5% disagreed with it and 6.25% were undecided about the issue.

From the above perspective it could be said that the federating states must posses adequate economic resources to support both an independent national government and independent regional governments. Both the central and the state governments should be economically autonomous for proper functioning of the federation. Hence, there is a need for restructuring of fiscal federalism in federalism in favour of states.

Industrial Development in India

A large number of industries have been established in the post-independent India in private, public and joint sectors. There are a lot of industrial resources and raw materials available in this country. Industrial towns like Bhilai, Rourkela, Ranchi, Jamshedpur, Renukoot are striking successes in this area. Despite these facts, there is very little industrialisation in India[5]. The argument centres around the security of the country. Self reliance in the case of defence materials as well as capital goods is essential both for reasons of security and for uninterrupted implementation of development plans.[6]

The planning commission of India has supported rapid industrialisation for rapid economic development by stressing that it would enhance labour productivity and help mobilise surpluses.[7]

Large-scale industries were started in the first fifteen years of planning in India. Rate of industrial growth was fluctuating between 2 and 12 percent. We observe a steady industrial progress was after 1967.[8] However, fluctuations continued to add to uncertainty. For example, in 1976-77 the industrial production increased at the rate of 9.6% to slide down by 1.4% in 1979-80, followed by an increase in 4% in 1980-81.[9]

Collaborations with industrially advanced countries like the USA, UK, USSR, France, Germany, Italy, Japan are a clear testimony of India's industrial progress.

Women administrators were asked to state whether "heavy industries are the only means to rapid economic growth". The results revealed that 6.25% of the respondents agreed with the view, while majority of them felt heavy industries are not the only means for economic growth. About 56.25% agreed and 18.75% strongly opposed the notion. There were almost 18.75% who could not express their opinion on this matter.

The women administrators reflected the government policy on industrialisation. The reason for the negative opinion was that small-scale industries are intended to fulfill and satisfy popular aspirations and relevant mundane requirements. Such industries could be set up at the very door step of the workers and it is also possible to resolve the problem of unemployment.

Role of Public Sector in Development

The public sector investments occupy an important place in India's economy. All major banks and insurance companies were nationalised in 1969 with a view to help the poor to realise the country's socialistic goals as stated in the constitution.

Due to the public sector investments, today India has made a noticeable progress, in steel, metallurgical mining, heavy engineering and electrical industries. The measure of public investment policy should be the rapid self-sustained economic development with 'distributive justice'.

The argument is that public enterprise generates surplus, creates job opportunities and promotes public welfare.[10] It restores economic health, supplements contribution and output of small-scale industries.[11] It assumes the role of model employer, encourages scientific exploitation of natural resources and conserves foreign exchange.[12] It consolidates efforts towards achieving society.[13] It rationalises the heights of the economy.[14] It is also held that the public sector prevents concentration of economic power in private hands.[15]

With the above notion the respondents were asked whether the "Growth of public sector could check the hold of monopolies in Indian economy".

Fig 6.1 shows that the respondents totally differed in their opinions about it. About 18.75% answered affirmatively and 6.25% strongly supported it, while 43.75% of them refuted the notion and 6.25% strongly opposed the notion of the role of public sectors. Nearly 25% of the respondents kept silent without giving their opinion.

However, it should be noted that the state in the capacity of an agent of social transformation through public expenditure on development is required to function as owner of resources and establishments, as a banker for investing finance through public sector corporations and undertakings and as manager of the public sector establishments. This triple alliance of owner, banker and manager facilitates coordination and proper communication in executing the public sector plans and proposals.

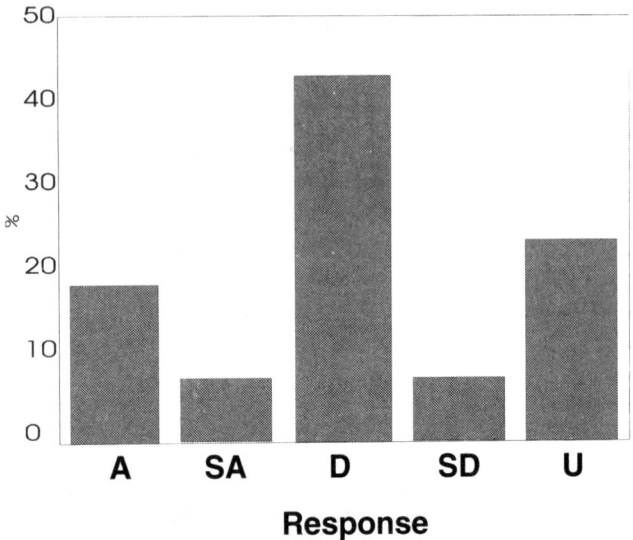

Fig. 6.1. Growth of Public Sectors Check Monopolies

A: Agree,

SA: Strongly Agree,

D: Disagree,

SD: Strongly Disagree,

U: Uncertain

Urban Property Ceiling

Ceiling on land holding relates to fixation of the maximum size of a holding that an individual cultivator or a household might possess. The basic objective of such a measure is to reduce disparities of income and wealth in the agrarian sector.[16]

Since urban land holding contributes much to the concentration of economic power, restrictions in that regard were welcome[17]. It is conceded that inequalities exist in the urban areas also which impede economic justice and welfare and negate objectives of socialistic pattern of society.[18] Since 17th February 1976, the urban land ceiling and regulation Act came into force.[19]

It is often stated that the ceiling on urban property, or any property is a violation of the fundamental rights. Right to property is one of the fundamental rights and it empowers every citizen to own the property for which he has put in labour, capital and skill. If ceiling on urban property is imposed, it would deprive the affected citizens of a fundamental right.

In this context, the respondents were asked to comment on the view that 'the provision of ceiling on urban property is against individuals 'fundamental rights'. Results revealed that 6.25% agreed and 6.25% strongly supported the view, while majority of the respondents 81.25% disapproved and 6.25% strongly opposed the view that land ceiling affects fundamental rights of citizens. Geetha Chaturvedi's study[20] also reveals that 80.8% executives and 64% educationists believed that provision of ceiling on urban property was definitely a step towards socialistic society and in way hampered fundamental rights.

Agricultural Land Ceiling

Laws on the ceiling of agricultural land, based on national guidelines, have been enacted and implemented in all the states except in Nagaland, Meghalaya, Arunachal Pradesh and Mizoram the land is generally held by the community. The objective of ceiling legislation has been to rationalise the policy, and its execution. Nevertheless, the pace of taking over and distribution of surplus land has been unsatisfactory.[21]

It has also been noted that the benefits of the Green Revolution and advanced agricultural technology have largely been appropriated by the emerging new process of economic growth[22].

Keeping in view the above notion on ceiling, the women executives were asked to express their opinion on the statement "Ceiling on agricultural land tends to reduce production". It could be true and 37.5% of them disapproved and 6.25% strongly refuted the statement. However, 37.5% did not comment on the notion.

In this context what is of greater concern is the fact that not much effort has been made to assist the allottees to develop the land[23]. Hence, it could be said that there is inadequate and inefficient administrative machinery and lukewarm attitude determination on the part of bureaucracy to implement land ceiling laws. There is enough evidence to show that, in actual operation, redistribution of land has become a marginal exercise.[24]

Heavy Taxation

The traditional view that every measure of old or new tax was an evil and each dose of public expenditure was a wastage, has undergone considerable change. There is also greater appreciation of the science of public finance, encompassing public expenditure, public debt and financial administration.[25]

In a developing economy, such as that of India, taxation is expected to perform at least three of the following functions: 1. To mobilise resources for economic development 2. To provide incentives for private investment; and 3. To reduce personal inequalities of wealth and income.

In the light of the aforesaid aspects, the respondents were asked whether "Heavy taxation is necessary for economic development of the country". None of the respondents agreed with the idea of heavy taxation. About 56.25% disapproved the idea. 18.75% strongly opposed it, while 25% were uncertain.

When compared with the responses of the women executives to the idea of progressive tax system, in Fig 6.2, it could be noted that the idea of imposing relatively heavier tax on the rich and a pattern of expenditure on the welfare schemes for the poor were favoured.

Therefore, it could be inferred that the respondents disapproved the idea of heavy taxation because when people are taxed heavily beyond the capacity of payment, they try to evade taxes.

Planning

Regarding the significance of planning, D.P. Mukerji[26] writes: "The plans means both a change of the axis of the ideal type of man and society as well as change of gear". Rationality is the key of planning. Planning seeks an adequate appreciation of new forces and their planned rational utilisation for national development. This could be achieved only by a popular, democratic, socialistic and welfare state.

Today planning has become a genuine instrument of economic and social change. The responsibility for formulation of a Five Year Plan lies with the Planning Commission of India which is headed by the prime minister as its chairman.

The respondents were asked whether planning in India should be totally decentralised in order to achieve the objectives of a welfare state. Fig. 6.2 shows that most of them seemed to be happy with the notion of decentralisation. About 56.25% agreed and 6.25% strongly approved the idea, while 25% of them disapproved it and 6.25% strongly opposed the notion. Nearly 6.25% were uncertain about the issue. When we compare Fig. 6.3 and Fig. 6.9 it could be said that most of the respondents favoured the idea of decentralisation.

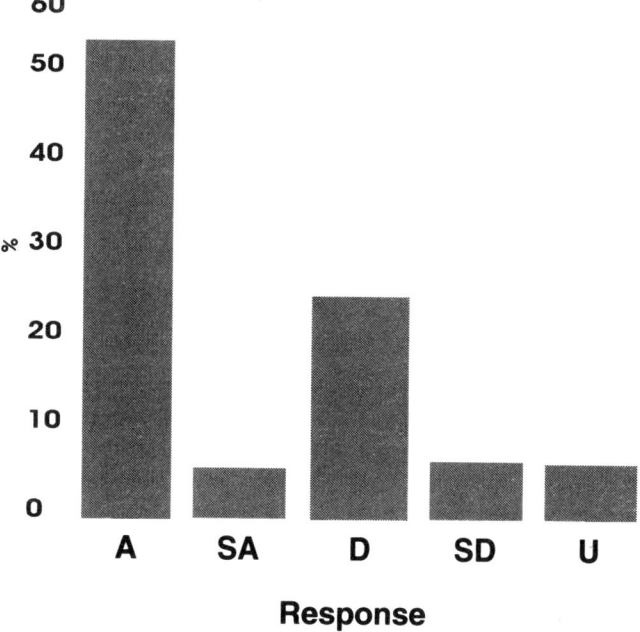

Fig. 6.2. Planning Should be Decentralised

A: Agree
SA: Strongly Agree
D: Disagree
SD: Strongly Disagree
U: Uncertain

Conclusion

The perspective of women administrators on economic development could be that mixed economy is suitable to India. The idea of progressive tax system and the fiscal federalism favouring the states were also supported by most of them.

Majority of the respondents felt heavy industries were not the only means for rapid economic growth. They favoured small scale industries instead of large scale industries as they felt small scale units would solve the problem of unemployment in India.

The respondents differed totally on the notion that growth of public sector could the hold of monopolies.

Majority of the executives felt that urban land ceiling does not affect the fundamental rights of the citizens. However, the view that ceiling on agricultural land tends to reduce production was fully accepted.

None of the respondents agreed with the notion of heavy taxation as it would lead to tax evasion. The idea of decentralisation of planning was supported by most of the women executives.

Notes and References

[1] Singh, Yogendra, "Concepts and Theories of Social Change", *A Survey of Research in Sociology and Social Anthropology*, Vol.I, Bombay: Popular Prakashan, 1974.
[2] Myrdal, Gunnar, *Asian Drama*, 3 Volumes., Penguin Books, 1968.
[3] Rao, V.K.R.V., *Essays on Economic Development*, Bombay: Asia Publishing House, 1964, p.34.
[4] Srivastava, L.N., *Comparative Political Systems – Theory and Practice of Modern Government*, Delhi: SBD Enterprises, 1988, p.155.
[5] Sharma, K.L., *Indian Society*, New Delhi: NCERT, 1990, p.159.
[6] Agarwal, A.N., *Indian Economy*, New Delhi: Vikas, 1980, p.381-383.
[7] Govt. of India, First Five Year Plan, New Delhi, 1982, p.3.
[8] Sharma, Op.cit., p.160.
[9] Economic Survey, *Financial Express*, 25 Feb., 1982, p.3.

[10] Ramaswamy, T., *Public Enterprises in India*, Delhi: Meenakshi Prakashan, 1972, p.58.
[11] Prakash, Jagadish, *Public Enterprises in India: A Study in Controls*, Allahabad Thinkers Library, 1980.
[12] Narain, Laxmi, *Principles and Practice of Public Enterprise Management*, New Delhi: S.Chand, 1980, p.51.
[13] Hanson, A.H., "Public Enterprise and Economic Development", London: Routledge & Kegan Paul Ltd, 1959, p.147.
[14] Desai, Morarji, "Public Sector in a Mixed Economy", Dagli Vadilal ed., *The Public Sector in India*, Bombay: Vora, 1969, p.1.
[15] Govt. of India, *Administrative Reforms Commission Report*, Public Sector Undertakings, Delhi", 1968, p.142.
[16] Chaturvedi, Geetha, *Women Administrators of India*, Jaipur: RBSA Publishers, p.9.
[17] Nangundappa, D.M., "Taxation of Urban Land", Brahamananda et al., ed., *Indian Economic Development and Policy*, New Delhi: Vikas, 1979, p.119.
[18] Lakshman, T.K."Economic Growth and Problem of Inequalities of Income", Brahmananda Corporation.,
[19] Dutt Ruddar and K.P.M. Sundharam, *Indian Economy*, New Delhi: S.Chand, 1979, p.309.
[20] Chaturvedi, Op.cit., p.151.
[21] Sixth Five Year Plan, p.114.
[22] Chaturvedi, Op.cit., p.114-115.
[23] Sixth Five Year Plan, p.114-115.
[24] Lakshman, Op.cit., p. 183.
[25] Elton, Hugh, *Principles of Public Finance*; Richard A. Musgrave, *The Theory of Public Finance*, New York: McGraw Hill, 1959.
[26] Mukerji, D.P., *Diversities*, New Delhi: People's Publishing House, 1958.

Conclusion and Suggestions

Socio-Economic Background

The choice of women administrators in Tamil Nadu was made with an idea to find out the nature of the problems they faced, the nature of discriminations they encountered and to compare their status and position with their less fortunate counterparts elsewhere. From the analysis of the socio-economic background of women administrators in Tamil Nadu it was found that the civil servants were of different age groups between 25 to 50 years. Their minimum years of experience was five and maximum above 25 years. As the age of the administrators increased the experience also increased. Most of the respondents were born in city and majority of them resided in urban setting. Those respondents who were born in cities chose their career because of the influence of parents, friends and due to their self-determination. Hence the city born respondents were comparatively more self-determined than the town born respondents. 75% of them belonged to forward castes and most of them were Hindus. There is a very low representation of lower castes and scheduled castes and no representation of scheduled tribes. Similarly Taub's study also revealed that among the IAS officers there were no representation of Sudras community. Hence it is clear that the representation of backward communities and especially SCs and STs continues to be low in IAS and IPS cadres. This is due to suppression of the SCs and STs in the Indian society. The respondents speak different languages like Marathi, Kashmiri, Hindi, Urdu, Telugu, Malayalam and Tamil as their mother tongue.

Nuclear family system is the prevalent family establishment while a few women live in joint families. They received their education from urban areas and all of them had their University education through English medium. Majority of them were postgraduates and their husbands were also postgraduates and administrators. In most cases the respondents' monthly income was above Rs. 7,000/- and their partners' income was also the same. The lowest income of respondents was Rs. 3,000/- to Rs. 4,000/-. It is also interesting to note that the younger respondents got higher income compared with the older respondents. This could be due to early entrance to the service by the younger respondents when compared to the older respondents and also due to the prevailing pay structure at that time.

Their fathers were postgraduates and professionals, or administrators or in government services while their mothers were matriculates and mostly housewives. 50% of the respondents considered both their and their husband's career as important while few of them felt that their career was more important than their partners'.

Administrators' Status at the Office

The respondents were found to be career ambitious and conscientious officers. They boldly gave suggestions to their superiors and most of them did not have any difficulty in working with their male superiors, colleagues and subordinates.

Generally, they were respected at work place because of their considerably higher rank and position. Their male superiors and colleague cooperated and adjusted with them and their male subordinates obeyed their orders without resistance. They were recognised and appreciated for the good work done and they were given full support by all the staff in their offices. This kind of peaceful environment gave the officers a high degree of job satisfaction. They were content with their profession and did not feel sorry for choosing the job. Even when they had excessive work to be accomplished, they willingly took their pending files home because they considered it as part of their duty.

Most of them felt that they did not suffer due to discrimination of sex, caste, religion or language. They could assert position while carrying out their work. More than 50% of the respondents felt that frequent transfers of administrators did not affect their efficiency and some of them did not have any kind of unpleasant experience in their service, while others had suffered difficult times on some occasions. It was the considered opinion of women administrators that civil services offered a promising pursuit of career for women and women officers should be given utmost encouragement.

Routine transfers being part of the system was considered a hindrance by several women administrators. Given their generalist background they were required to serve in diverse capacities and sectors. It was their view that constant changes of assignments seriously affected their assignments that they were handling. This dampened their zeal, devotion and commitment to their profession. In fact, it had encouraged a level of complacency in the administrators.

The respondents wanted to preserve their autonomy while enjoying their accessibility to the public. This autonomy and accessibility provides a vital aspect for the healthy functioning of any system, and helps in the effective disposal of cases and efficient tackling of problems and complications.

Autonomy of actions was an important fact that all the respondents reiterated in emphatic terms. The constant interference of politicians, MLAs and the political parties in general greatly hampered their determined and serious efforts. The need was to reduce and eliminate unwarranted political interference that was detrimental to effective administrative action. Objectivity and political restructuring were the most important factors in policy formulation and implementation that would promote the best interests of the larger public and the administration.

Administrators' Status within their Families

The respondents were queried on their domestic responsibilities and official duties and their approaches to problems they faced in their sectors. Because of their important positions as responsible administrative executives of the state and the nature of their responsibilities, they were expected to devote all their energies and attention to that pursuit. Equally demanding was the domestic front where responsibilities still lay with regard to family maintenance, child care, and household responsibilities. The pressures of the work greatly reduced the time at their disposal for their respective households. Thus, it is evident that administrative responsibilities of the state overwhelmed their domestic commitments.

In some families, the Indian tradition of females eating after the male members and the preferential treatment given to boys was still followed. Nearly 50% of the respondents had time to entertain their friends and guests at home while others did not find time and few others did not like to mingle with the public. For some non-Tamil speaking respondents, language acted as a barrier in working effectively.

50% of them could not afford to spend time in fulfilling their responsibilities at home due to lack of time and also due to the nature of the job they were holding. It was here that the crucial support of their spouses made the difference. They willingly shared their responsibilities. The women officers did not suffer like other women at their homes.

Women administrators enjoyed equally congenial atmosphere at home as they enjoyed in their office. In keeping with their official status they enjoyed considerable freedom at home in all matters of family administration.

In several aspects the women executives enjoyed equality of status along with their spouses. Decisions made on family matters were effected in harmony and cooperation, the two understanding each other's needs, status and desires.

Attitudes towards Social Change

The next aspect of enquiry focused on the respondents' perspectives on the various contentions, socio-economic and political issues. The unanimous view was that social change of dramatic dimensions and comprehensive scope was the need of the hour. It must be effected without further loss of time to better the lives and the lot of Indian women. Their views were in the following lines.

Despite the advancement of literacy and the increased social and civil awareness, evils of dowry, casteism, child-marriage, exploitation, prostitution unemployment, exploitation of the figure of women by the media were the continuing order of the day.

Education and empowerment could alone be the effective antidotes to these problems. Effective legislation and its stringent implementation should be accompanied by other positive measures for meaningful results. A certain level of scepticism was also prevalent among them. Some of the respondents were of the view that these anticipated social changes would not be quick and smooth in view of the reality of social rigidity.

Indian social reality accepts the dominance of the masculine gender. It has always glorified the virtues of boyhood and eventually manhood and has identified this symbol with success, strength and achievement. Psychologically the complexities of masculine superiority and feminine inferiority conditions the Indian psyche. Harassments at all levels culminate in marriage and the issue of dowry. The Indian women is the target of attack, scorn and derision by her spouse and her in-laws. The incessant psychological pressure with the accompanying inferiority complex stereotyping wrecks her personality. Never in her life in the premarital stage (dependent on parents) has she the opportunity to enjoy to the free air of independence.

Dowry and gifts are quantified on the basis of their monetary value. The value of the girl is assessed on the basis of the wealth which she brings. The varying degrees of the distresses of the Indian woman are directly proportionate to the relative value of the dowry factor which is an intricate inevitable causal factor of Indian marriage system. Hence, the notion of equality of status is a misnomer despite any level of education and enlightenment. This problem is specially seen even among the educated sections of the society.

The significant attitudes of women administrators towards social change are as follows. The respondents wanted to have equal status with men and also equal share in property. All of them felt that dowry lowers the status of women. Casteism was considered as a negative factor affecting the development of the nation. Majority of them wanted 21 years to be fixed as the minimum age for marriage even for girls. Most of them felt that the girls should have at least higher secondary education. The majority of the respondents felt that the problem of unemployment was not due to the fact that many women started taking up jobs. All of them disapproved with the reservation policy in India. All the respondents believed that coeducation helps to bridge the gap between both the sexes. Legalisation of abortion was a controversial view among the respondents. None of them agreed that belief in God reflects the weak personality of the person. They accepted that religion and morality are related to each other. They also believed in fatalism. The problem of increase in cases of AIDS was attributed to immoral traffic of women. They even opposed legalisation of prostitution. The exploitation of the image of women by the media was resented by most of them. All the respondents did not consider sex determination test as a threat to women. Most of them felt that economic independency of women elevated their status. The general view of respondents was that active participation in politics did not necessarily uplift the status of women. The majority of women officers felt that recognition of their official positions elevated their domestic status. According to most of the women administrators, the social inequalities faced by women in India have neutralised their constitutional and legal rights.

Opinion about the Political System

The political views of the women administrators are significant because of their place in the administrative system.

Most respondents strongly felt that democracy was the most suitable system of governance for India. The democratic structure should be strengthened through considerable changes in the electoral system. Proportional representation of minorities including women should be reinforced in democracy. Their ideological views on the nature of socialism and democracy were significant. They strongly felt that failure of the judiciary and an active institution has been the greatest setback to the Indian democratic enterprise. 80% of the respondents favoured equal representation from all social and economic classes.

Merit of the candidates should be the sole criterion for recruitment. They were against the idea of specific task allotments to women and instead preferred the jurisdiction as the most viable administrative unit. They were all against the right of civil servants resorting to strike as a means of bargain with the government.

Some even advocated special reservation for women in legislature. Free media was commended by one and all.

Perspective on Economic Development

The perspective of women administrators on economic development was that mixed economy with the progressive tax system and fiscal federalism favouring the states was suitable to the Indian set-up. Most of them felt that heavy industries are not the only means for rapid economic growth. They favoured small-scale industries instead of large-scale industries as small-scale units would reduce the unemployment problem in India.

The notion that growth of public sector would check the hold of monopolies was not accepted by the respondents. Majority of the executives felt that urban land ceiling does not affect the fundamental rights of citizens. The view that ceiling on agricultural land tends to reduce production was not accepted by all. None agreed with the heavy taxation policy and decentralisation of planning was supported by most of them.

SUGGESTIONS

The following suggestions emerge out of the above analysis. Emancipation of women being the main issue certain pragmatic measures should be meaningfully implemented.

(a) All efforts should be undertaken towards the positive development of the girl child. Focusing on her education, health, and status, proper measures should be taken for their nurture and upbringing. Increased social awareness of their problems should be brought about. Encouraging women to take up higher studies and motivating them to opt for the civil services are the first measures to be taken as social respectability emerges from educational attainment and economic independence.

(b) Education of the girl child as a special policy should be formulated by Union Ministry of Human Resources Development/Social Welfare. Encouragement should be given to them to compete in career oriented examinations like the Union Public Service Commission, Staff Selection Commission, Bank Examinations. Special coaching facilities for the rural women candidates, women candidates of the first generation learners should be effectively implemented.

(c) A master plan in this regard should be formulated at the Union Government level and should be effected as a mandatory reform in the states. Women candidates especially belonging to the backward classes, scheduled castes and scheduled tribes should be given encouragement under the above master plan to effect a meaningful development.

(d) Women must be educated about women's rights, human rights, and the constitutional provisions. They must be encouraged to cope with stress both in office and while fulfilling family responsibilities.

(e) Women of younger generation should be encouraged to have self-introspection, realise their deficiencies, improve their will power, determination and self-confidence. With the support of families, society and government, women could easily take up challenges in the higher posts.

(f) Government should conduct gender sensitisation programmes to encourage the society to frame future goals and visions for improving the status of women.

(g) Girls must be encouraged right from the childhood days to have women role models who have achieved something in life.

(h) The age old Indian tradition of suppressing the girl child and the outcasts should be discouraged by giving more educational opportunities to them. If the present generation is educated then the future generation will be able to achieve 100% literacy and the present problems will be gradually eradicated.

(i) The representation of women in administration should be increased because firstly, it is the democratic and constitutional right of women. Secondly, women administrators could understand women's issues and problems of other women better. Thirdly, women police officers could stringently check and control crime against women. Fourthly, they could formulate pro-women and women friendly policies. Fifthly, as 50% of India's population are women, it is necessary that more women should be allowed in the policy-making process.

(j) Women police officers should exclusively handle cases of innocent women suffering in prison. Interference by male officers in the trial of such cases should be stopped to ensure discrimination and bias against women.

(k) Development programmes for women in the states should be formulated and meaningfully implemented. Care must be taken that such programmes are assigned to women administrators with commitment, as that would ensure the fullest benefit reaching the appropriate clientele.

(l) Posting of women officers with their spouses should be made mandatory. Outstation transfers if necessitated should be done in such a way that they don't lead to hardships.

(m) A separate cell exclusively devoted to the problems of women administrators at all levels should be established to look into the professional spheres. This cell would function as a counselling centre for all women executives.

(n) Women officers should take extra efforts to improve public relations and gain people's support for the policies formulated for the progress of women.

(o) Women executives should have their own networking to develop personal and professional skills for their own advancement and take extra strategic efforts to increase the number of women in the civil services.

(p) Women administrators should perform better than their male counterparts and highlight their success stories to the public to deconstruct the myths about inabilities of women to shoulder responsibilities and tough jobs like police.

Therefore, it could be said that the immediate need of the hour in the new millennium is that the women administrators who are already holding top positions in the government should realise that their prime duty is to bring overall development of women and improve the status of women in India.

Lastly, the only option to increase the representation of women in civil services is to give reservation in order to encourage more and more number of women to appear for UPSC exams.

With regard to further research in this field, one can undoubtedly say that it is a fertile soil for further research and investigation. The future researchers may compare the male and female administrators in the state of Tamil Nadu.

Bibliography

PRIMARY SOURCES

Reports

1. Government of India, First Five Year Plan, New Delhi: 1952.
2. Report of the Suicide Enquiry Committee Pushapaben, Government of Gujarat, 1964.
3. Government of India, "Administrative Reforms Commission Report: Public Sector Undertakings" 1968.,
4. Sixth Five Year Plan, (1980-85).
5. *Women in Tamil Nadu- A Profile*, The Tamil Nadu Corporation for Development of Women Ltd, Madras, 1986.
6. A synopsis of the report of the National Committee on Status of Women in India, *ICSSR*, New Delhi, 1988.
7. Brief analysis of provisional census figures, 1991.
8. Provisional population total: India, 2001 Census results.

Encyclopaedia:

1. *The New Encyclopaedia Britannica*, Micropaedia, 15th Edition, Volume 9.

Newspapers:

1. *Indian Express*, Editorial, 27th April, 1984.
2. Economic Survey, *Financial Express*, 25th February, 1982.
3. *Employment News*, 17-23 October, 1992.
4. *Employment News*, 11-17 February, 1995.

SECONDARY SOURCES:

1. Agarwal, A.N., *Indian Economy*, New Delhi: Vikas Publishing House (Pvt.) Ltd., 1980.
2. Almond, G.A. and G.B. Powell (Jr), *Comparative Politics: A Development Approach*, New Delhi: Amerind Publishing Co (P) Ltd, 1972.
3. Avasthi, Amreshwar and Anand Prakash Avasthi, *Public Administration in India*, 7th Revised Edition, Agra: Lakshmi Narain Agarwal, 2001.
4. Beteille, A., *Caste, Class and Power*, New Delhi: Oxford University Press, 1972.
5. Bette Ann Stead, *Women in Management*, 2nd Ed., N.J.: Prentice Hall, Inc. Englewood Cliffs, 1985.
6. Bhambhri, C.P., *Administrators in a Changing Society*: New Delhi: National Publishing House, 1972.
7. Blunt, E.A.H., *The Indian Civil Service*, London: Faber and Faber, 1937.
8. Chaturvedi. G., *The Administrator of India*, Jaipur: RBSA Publications, 1985.
9. Crozier, M., *The Bureaucratic Phenomenon*, Chicago: University Press of Chicago, 1964.
10. Desai, M., "Public Sector in a Mixed Economy," in Vadilal Dagli ed., *The Public Sector in India*, Vora: Bombay, 1969.
11. Desai, N. and M., Krishnaraj, *Women and Society in India*, Ajantha Publications, Delhi, 1987.
12. Desai, N. and V. Patel, *Indian Women Change and Challenge in the International Decade 1975-85*, Bombay: Popular Prakashan Pvt. Ltd, Bombay, 1990
13. Devasundaram, S., "Roots of Suppression of Women in India," Bangalore: CSI Women's Fellowship, 1992.
14. Dutt, R., and K.P.M. Sundharam, *Indian Economy*: New Delhi: and Co. (Pvt.) Ltd., 1979.

15. Elton, H., *Principles of Public Finance*, and Richard A. Musgrave, *The Theory of Public Finance*, New York: Mc Graw Hill, 1959.
16. Epostein, C.F., *Women's Place, Options and Limits in Professional Careers*, University of California Press, 1973.
17. Everett, J., "Women in Law and Administration" in Jana Everett., Lebra and Joy Paulson ed., *Women and Work: Continuity and Change*, New Delhi: Promilla and Co. Publications, 1984.
18. Forbes, G. "The Indian Women's Movement: Struggle for Women's Right of National Liberation in the Extended Family," *Women and Political Participation in India and Pakistan*, edited by Gail Minault, Delhi: Chanakya Publications, 1981.
19. Fredda, Brilliant, *Women in Power*, New Delhi: Lancer International, 1987.
20. Gandhi, M.K., *Women and Social Injustice*, Ahmedabad: Navjivan Publishing House, 1947.
21. Ghandiall, R., *Women in Indian Society*, New Delhi: Sage Publications, 1988.
22. Goode, W.J., *Why Men Resist in Rethinking the Family: Some Feminist Questions*, ed. by Barrie Thorne and Marilyn Yalom, Orient Longman, 1982.
23. Govrour, H., *The Captive Wife*, London: Routledge and Kegan Paul, 1966.
24. Hanson, A.H., *Public Enterprise and Economic Development*, London: Routledge and Kegan Paul Ltd, 1959.
25. Kapadia, K.M., *Marriage and Family in India*, Calcutta: Oxford University Press, 1964.
26. Kapur, P., *Marriage and the Working Women in India*, New Delhi: Vikas Publishing, House, 1972.
27. Kapur, P., *Love, Marriage and Sex*, Vikas Publishing House 1974.
28. Karve, I., *Kinship Organisation in India*, 3rd Edition, Bombay: Asia Publishing House, 1968.

29. Khanna, G., and M.A. Vaeghese, *Indian Women Today*, New Delhi: Vikas Publications, 1978.
30. Kothari, R., *Caste in Indian Politics*, New Delhi: Orient Longman, 1970.
31. Kulkarni, M.G., *Family Research in India: Retrospect and Prospect*, Delhi: B.R. Publishing Corporation, 1982.
32. Krisonswadi, N., *Women Executives – A Sociological Study in Role Income*, Jaipur: Rawat Publications, 1989.
33. Lakshman, T.K., *Economic Growth and Problem of Inequalities of Income*, Delhi: Brahmananda Corporation, , 1982.
34. Lalitha Devi, V., *Status and Employment of Women in India*, Delhi: B.R. Publishing Corporation, 1982.
35. Louis, M.J., *An Inquiry into the Background and Status of Women Executives*, Madurai: The Modern Printers, 1990.
36. Mahadevan, A., *Women and Population Dynamics – Perspectives from Asian Countries*, New Delhi: Sage Publications, 1989.
37. Mahajan, A., *Indian Policewomen*, New Delhi: Deep & Deep Publications, 1982.
38. Majumdar,V., *Another Development with Women : A View from Asian in Development Dialogue*, Uppsala: The Dag Hammarskjold Foundation, 1982.
39. Malley, L.S.S.O, *The India Civil Service : 1601-1930*, London: Frank Cass & Co, 1965.
40. Mehta,V., *Attitude of Educated Women towards Social Issues*, New Delhi: National Publishing House, 1979.
41. Merton, R., *Bureaucratic Structure and Personality in Social Theory and Social Structure*, New York: Free Press of Glence, Inc., 1949.
42. Misra, B.B., *The Bureaucracy in India – An Historical Analysis of Development upto 1947*, Delhi: Oxford University Press, 1980.

43. Misra, B.B., *Government and Bureaucracy in India : 1947-1976*: Delhi: Oxford University Press, 1986.
44. Morse, C., et al. (ed), *Modernisation by Design*, Calcutta: Scientific Book Agency, 1972.
45. Mukerji, D.P., *Diversities*, New Delhi: People's Publishing House, , 1958.
46. Myrdal, G. *Asian Drama*, 3rd Volume, Penguin Books, 1968.
47. Nanjundappa, D.M., "Taxation of Urban Land," in Brahmananda et. al, ed., *Indian Economic Development and Policy*, New Delhi: Vikas Publishing House, 1979.
48. Narain, D., ed. *Explorations in the Family and Other Essays*, Bombay: T. Thacker & Co, 1975.
49. Narain, L. *Principles and Practice of Public Enterprise Management*, New Delhi: S.Chand, 1980.
50. Nettle, J.P., and Roland, R., *International System and the Modernisation of Societies*, London: Faber & Faber, 1968.
51. Pandey, S., *Women in Politics*, Jaipur, Rawat Publications, 1990.
52. Parikh, I.J., and P.K. Garg, *Indian Women – An Inner Dialogue*, Sage Publications: New Delhi, 1989.
53. Park, R. L., and Bueno. B. de Mesquita, *India's Political System*, New Jersey: Prentice Hall, 1979.
54. Patel, V., "Sex Determination and Sex Preselection Tests: Abuse of Advanced Technologies", in Rehana Ghandiall ed., *Women in Indian Society*, New Delhi: Sage Publications, 1985.
55. Prakash, J., *Public Enterprises in India: A Study in Controls*, Library: Allahabad, Thinkers 1980.
56. Mishra, Pramod and Urmila Mahopatra, *Women Administrators and Professionals: A Global Perspective*, Delhi: Kalinga Publications, 2003
57. Kumar, Raman, *Women Executives*, New Delhi: Deep & Deep Publications, 1993.

58. Ramaswamy, T., *Public Enterprises in India*, New Delhi: Meenakshi Prakashan, 1972.
59. Rao, V.K.R.V., *Essays in Economic Development*, Bombay: Asia Publishing House, 1964.
60. Rudolph, L.I., and S.H., Rudolph, *The Modernity of Indian Tradition: Political Development in India*, New Delhi: Orient Longman, 1969.
61. Sahai, N., "Women in Administration: A Growing Phenomenon" *Directory of Indian Women Today*, New Delhi: India International Publishers, 1976.
62. Buddapriya, Sangamitra, *Women in Management*, New Delhi: A.P.H. Publishing Corporation, 1999
63. Sengupta, P., *Women Workers of India*, Bombay: Asia Publishing House, 1960.
64. Aleem, Shamim, *Women in Indian Police*, Sterling Publishers Ltd. 1991.
65. Aleem, Shamim, *Women Police and Social Change*, New Delhi: Ashish Publishing House, 1991.
66. Kohli Chandra, Shanta, *A Study of Women in Administration: A Situational Analysis*, New Delhi: Radha Publications, 1997.
67. Sharma, K.L., *Indian Society*, New Delhi: NCERT, 1990.
68. Sharma, R.K., *Nationalism, Social Reform and Indian Women*, New Delhi: Janaki Prakashan, 1981.
69. Singh, Y., *Concepts and Theories of Social Change: A Survey of Research in Sociology and Social Anthropology*, Volume I, Bombay: Popular Prakashan, 1964.
70. Singi, N.K., *Bureaucracy: Positions and Persons*, New Delhi: Abhinav Publishing House, 1974.
71. Sinha, V.M., *Women and Violence*, New Delhi: Vikas Publishing House Pvt. Ltd. 1989.

72. Sinha, V.M., "The Superior Civil Services in India – A Study in Administrative Development (1947-1957)," *IRAS*, Jaipur, 1985.

73. Srinivas, M.N., *Caste in Modern India and Other Essays*, Bombay: Media Promoters and Publishers Pvt. Ltd, 1978.

74. Srivastava, L.N., *Comparative Political Systems – Theory and Practice of Modern Government*, Delhi: SBD Enterprises, 1988.

75. Subramanium, V., *Social Background of India's Administrators*, Ministry of Broadcasting, New Delhi Publications Division, 1971.

76. Taub, R. P., *Bureaucrats under Stress: Administrators and Administration in an Indian State*, firma, K.L. Mukhopadhyay, Calcutta, 1969.

77. Verba, S., B. Ahmed, and A. Bhatt, *Caste, Race and Politics*, Sage Publications: Beverly Hills, 1971.

78. Wal, S., and Shruti Banerji, *Encyclopedia of Women as Human Resource in 21st Century and Beyond*, Vol-I, 'Women in Developing World', Institute for Integrated Society Development, Lucknow, Sarup & Sons, New Delhi, 2001.

79. Wal, S. and Shruti Banerji, *Encyclopedia of Women as Human Resource in 21st Century and Beyond*, Vol-II, *Women as Productive Humane Resource*, Institute for Integrated Society Development, Lucknow, Sarup & Sons, New Delhi, 2001.

80. Wal, S., and Shruti Banerji, *Encyclopedia of Women as Human Resource in 21st Century and Beyond*, Vol-III, *Women in Decision Making*, Institute for Integrated Society Development, Lucknow, Sarup & Sons, New Delhi, 2001.

81. Wal, S., and Shruti Banerji, *Encyclopedia of Women as Human Resource in 21st Century and Beyond*, Vol-IV, *Women and Gobalization*, Institute for Integrated Society Development, Lucknow, Sarup & Sons, New Delhi, 2001.

82. Weiner, M., *Politics of Scarcity*, Chicago: University Press of Chicago, 1962.

83. Zweig, F., *Women's Life and Labour*, London: Gollanez, 1952.

ARTICLES AND JOURNALS

1. Kelkar, Govind., "Violence against Women: An Understanding of Responsibility for their lives", *Samya Shakti, A Journal of Women's Studies*, 2, no. 1, 1985.
2. Misra, B.B., "Evolution of the Office of Collector", *Indian Journal of Public Administration*, July-September, 1965.
3. Ray, N.K., "Women's Role in National Development: Documentation on Women's concerns", Library and Documentation Centre, New Delhi, All India Association for Christian Higher Education, October to December, 1991.
4. Richard, H.Hall, "Intra Organisational Structural Variation : Application of the Bureaucratic Model", *Administrative Science Quarterly 7*, no. 3, 1962.
5. Jolly, Sushma, "Women : Too Soft for Politics", *Femina*, July, 1982.

UNPUBLISHED PAPERS

1. Sayeed, Badar, "Property Rights and Women," (Unpublished) Paper, *PENN*, Centre for Women's Studies, Madras.
2. Kum Kum, Kishore "Women in India Administrative Services," Ph.D. Thesis (Unpublished), Banaras Hindu University, 1986.
3. Dasgupta, Sugata, "Emancipation of Women in India," (Unpublished paper) prepared for the committee on the status of women in India.

Map 1

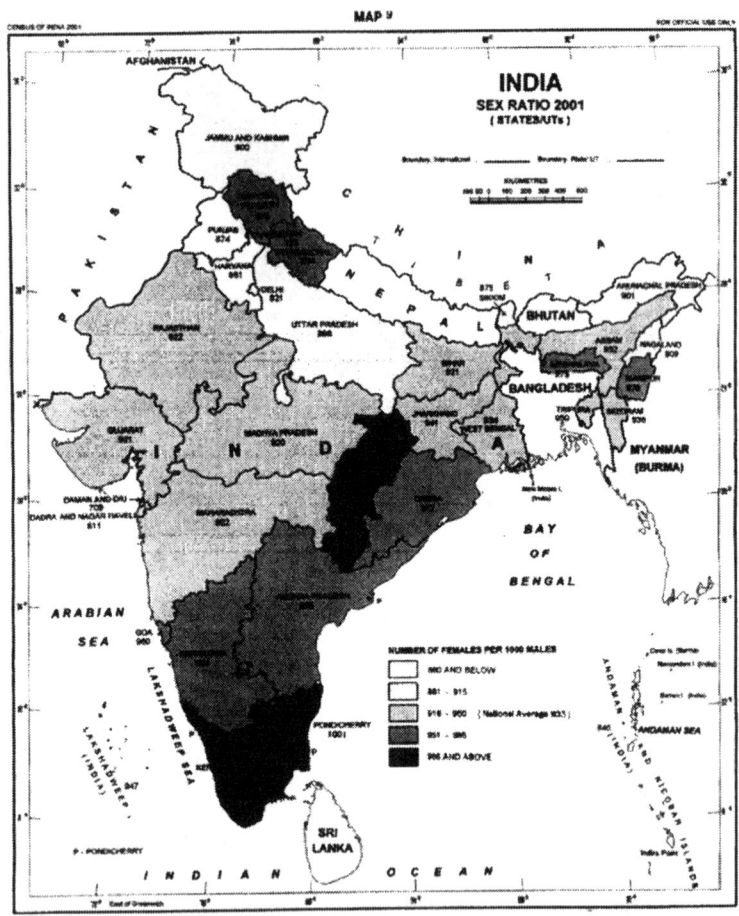

Map 2

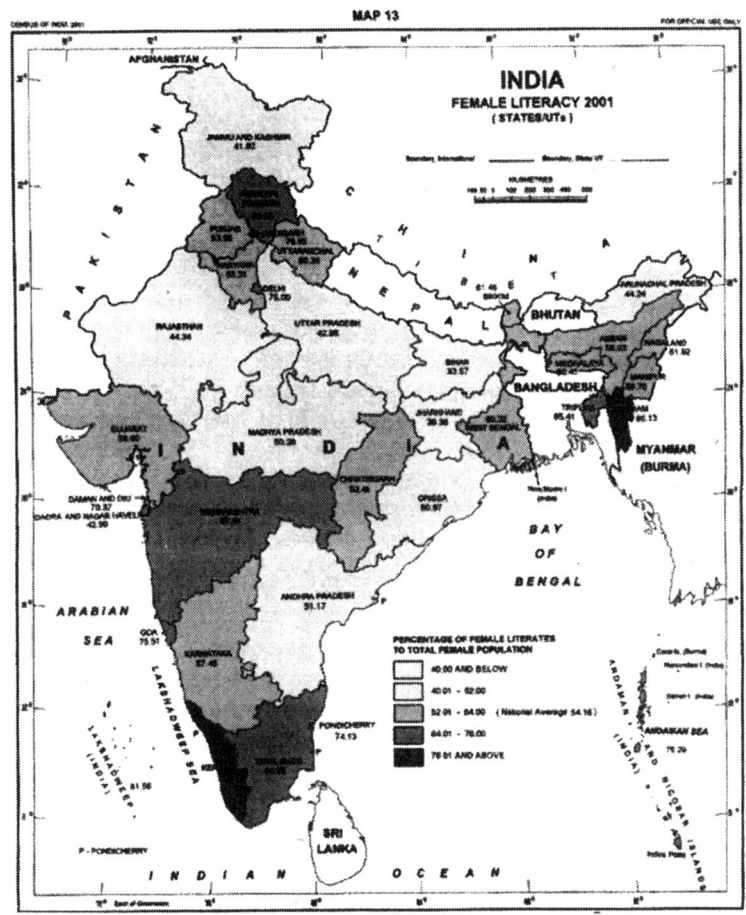

Table 1

Census of India 2001

Sl. No.	India/State/Union territories*	POPULATION			Population Variation 1991 - 2001	Sex ratio (females per thousand males)
		PERSONS	MALES	FEMALES		
	INDIA 1,2	1,027,015,247	531,277,078	495,738,169	21.34	933
1	Andaman & Nicobar Is.*	356,265	192,985	163,280	26.94	846
2	Andhra Pradesh	75,727,541	38,286,811	37,440,730	13.86	978
3	Arunachal Pradesh	1,091,117	573,951	517,166	26.21	901
4	Assam	26,638,407	13,787,799	12,850,608	18.85	932
5	Bihar	82,878,796	43,153,964	39,724,832	28.43	921
6	Chandigarh*	900,914	508,224	392,690	40.33	773
7	Chhatisgarh	20,795,956	10,452,426	10,343,530	18.06	990
8	Dadra & Nagar Haveli*	220,451	121,731	98,720	59.20	811
9	Daman & Diu*	158,059	92,478	65,581	55.59	709
10	Delhi*	13,782,976	7,570,890	6,212,086	46.31	821
11	Goa	1,343,998	685,617	658,381	14.89	960
12	Gujarat 5	50,596,992	26,344,053	24,252,939	22.48	921
13	Haryana	21,082,989	11,327,658	9,755,331	28.06	861
14	Himachal Pradesh 4	6,077,248	3,085,256	2,991,992	17.53	970
15	Jammu & Kashmir 2,3	10,069,917	5,300,574	4,769,343	29.04	900
16	Jharkhand	26,909,428	13,861,277	13,048,151	23.19	941
17	Karnataka	52,733,958	26,856,343	25,877,615	17.25	964
18	Kerala	31,838,619	15,468,664	16,369,955	9.42	1,058
19	Lakshadweep*	60,595	31,118	29,477	17.19	947
20	Madhya Pradesh	60,385,118	31,456,873	28,928,245	24.34	920
21	Maharashtra	96,752,247	50,334,270	46,417,977	22.57	922
22	Manipur	2,388,634	1,207,338	1,181,296	30.02	978
23	Meghalaya	2,306,069	1,167,840	1,138,229	29.94	975
24	Mizoram	891,058	459,783	431,275	29.18	938
25	Nagaland	1,988,636	1,041,686	946,950	64.41	909
26	Orissa	36,706,920	18,612,340	18,094,580	15.94	972
27	Pondicherry*	973,829	486,705	487,124	20.56	1,001
28	Punjab	24,289,296	12,963,362	11,325,934	19.76	874

29	Rajasthan	56,473,122	29,381,657	27,091,465	28.33	922
30	Sikkim	540,493	288,217	252,276	32.98	875
31	Tamil Nadu	62,110,839	31,268,654	30,842,185	11.19	986
32	Tripura	3,191,168	1,636,138	1,555,030	15.74	950
33	Uttar Pradesh	166,052,859	87,466,301	78,586,558	25.80	898
34	Uttaranchal	8,479,562	4,316,401	4,163,161	19.20	964
35	West Bengal	80,221,171	41,487,694	38,733,477	17.84	934

Notes:

1. The population of India includes the estimated population of entire Kachchh district, Morvi, Maliya-Miyana and Wankaner talukas of Rajkot district, Jodiya taluka of Jamanagar district of Gujarat State and entire Kinnaur district of Himachal Pradesh where population enumeration of Census of India 2001 could not be conducted due to natural calamity.
2. For working out density of India, the entire area and population of those portions of Jammu and Kashmir which are under illegal occupation of Pakistan and China have not been taken into account.
3. Figures shown against Population in the age-group 0-6 do not include the figures of entire Kachchh district, Morvi, Maliya-Miyana and Wankaner talukas of Rajkot district, Jodiya taluka of Jamanagar district and entire Kinnaur district of Himachal Pradesh where population enumeration of Census of India 2001 could not be conducted due to natural calamity.
4. Figures shown against Himachal Pradesh have been arrived at after including the estimated figures of entire Kinnaur district of Himachal Pradesh where the population enumeration of Census of India 2001 could not be conducted due to natural calamity.
5. Figures shown against Gujarat have been arrived at after including the estimated figures of entire Kachchh district, Morvi, Maliya-Miyana and Wankaner talukas of Rajkot district, Jodiya taluka of Jamanagar district of Gujarat State where the population enumeration of Census of India 2001 could not be conducted due to natural calamity.

(Source: *Provisional Population Totals : India* . Census of India 2001, Paper 1 of 2001)

Table 2

Census of India 2001

	STATE	LITERACY RATE (2001 Census) (in %)			LITERACY RATE (1991 Census)	CHANGE IN LITERACY RATE (1991-2001)
		PERSONS	MALES	FEMALES		
	INDIA 1	65.38	75.96	54.28	51.63	13.75
1	Andaman & Nicobar Is.*	81.18	86.07	75.29	73.02	8.17
2	Andhra Pradesh	61.11	70.85	51.17	44.09	17.02
3	Arunachal Pradesh	54.74	64.07	44.24	41.59	13.15
4	Assam	64.28	71.93	56.03	52.89	11.52
5	Bihar	47.53	60.32	33.57	37.49	10.04
6	Chandigarh*	81.76	85.65	76.65	77.81	3.94
7	Chhatisgarh	65.18	77.86	52.40	42.91	22.27
8	Dadra & Nagar Haveli*	60.03	73.32	42.99	40.71	19.33
9	Daman & Diu*	81.09	88.40	70.37	71.20	9.89
10	Delhi*	81.82	87.37	75.00	75.29	6.53
11	Goa	82.32	88.88	75.51	75.51	6.81
12	Gujarat	69.97	80.50	58.60	61.29	8.68
13	Haryana	68.59	79.25	56.31	55.85	12.74
14	Himachal Pradesh	77.13	86.02	68.08	63.86	13.27
15	Jammu & Kashmir	54.46	65.75	41.82	NA	NA
16	Jharkhand	54.13	67.94	39.38	41.39	12.74
17	Karnataka	67.04	76.29	57.45	56.04	11.00
18	Kerala	90.92	94.20	87.86	89.81	1.11
19	Lakshadweep *	87.52	93.15	81.56	81.78	5.74
20	Madhya Pradesh	64.11	76.80	50.28	44.67	19.41
21	Maharashtra	77.27	86.27	67.51	64.87	12.39
22	Manipur	68.87	77.87	59.70	59.89	8.97
23	Meghalaya	63.31	66.14	60.41	49.10	14.21
24	Mizoram	88.49	90.69	86.13	82.27	6.22
25	Nagaland	67.11	71.77	61.92	61.65	5.45
26	Orissa	63.61	75.95	50.97	49.09	14.52
27	Pondicherry*	81.49	88.89	74.13	74.74	6.74
28	Punjab	69.95	75.63	63.55	58.51	11.45

29	Rajasthan	61.03	76.46	44.34	38.55	22.48
30	Sikkim	69.68	76.73	61.46	56.94	12.61
31	Tamil Nadu	73.47	82.33	64.55	62.66	10.81
32	Tripura	73.66	81.47	65.41	60.44	13.22
33	Uttar Pradesh	57.36	70.23	42.98	40.71	16.65
34	Uttaranchal	72.28	84.01	60.26	57.75	14.53
35	West Bengal	69.22	77.58	60.22	57.70	11.52

Notes:

1. The population of India includes the estimated population of entire Kachchh district, Morvi, Maliya-Miyana and Wankaner talukas of Rajkot district, Jodiya taluka of Jamanagar district of Gujarat State and entire Kinnaur district of Himachal Pradesh where population enumeration of Census of India 2001 could not be conducted due to natural calamity.
2. Figures shown against and literates do not include the figures of entire Kachchh district, Morvi, Maliya-Miyana and Wankaner talukas of Rajkot district, Jodiya taluka of Jamanagar district and entire Kinnaur district of Himachal Pradesh where population enumeration of Census of India 2001 could not be conducted due to natural calamity.
3. Figures shown against Himachal Pradesh have been arrived at after including the estimated figures of entire Kinnaur district of Himachal Pradesh where the population enumeration of Census of India 2001 could not be conducted due to natural calamity.

(Source: *Provisional Population Totals : India* . Census of India 2001, Paper 1 of 2001)

Table 3

Provisional Population Totals: TAMIL NADU

The total population of Tamil Nadu as at 0:00 hours of 1st March 2001 stood at 62,110,839 as per the provisional results of the Census of India 2001. In terms of population it holds the sixth position among the States and Union territories in the country. As against all India decadal growth rate of population 21.34% during 1991-2001, in Tamil Nadu this has further slipped to 11.19% from 15.39% during 1981-1991. The sex ratio (i.e., the number of females per thousand males) of population in the State has improved from 974 in the previous census to 986 in the present census. The literacy rate in the State has shown remarkable improvement. This has increased to 73.47% when compared to 62.66% ten years back during 1991 Census.

Population:

Persons	62,110,839
Males	31,268,654
Females	30,842,185

Sex Ratio: 986

Population (0 - 6 years):

Persons	6,817,669
Males	3,515,562
Females	3,302,107

Sex Ratio: 939

Number of Literates:

Persons	40,624,398
Males	22,847,735
Females	17,776,663

Decadal Growth 1991 - 2001:

Persons :   (+) 11.19 %
Male   :   (+) 10.49 %
Females :   (+) 11.91 %

Percentage of Population (0-6) to Total Population:

Persons :   10.98 %
Males   :   11.24 %
Females :   10.71 %

Percentage of Literates to Total Population:

Persons :   73.47 %
Males   :   82.33 %
Females :   64.55 %

(Source: *Provisional Population Totals : India*. Census of India 2001, Paper 1 of 2001)

Index

AIDS, 139
   and immorality, 98, 103
   problems of, 98
Abortion, 139
   and termination of unwanted pregnancy, 96-97
   legalisation of, 96, 103
   Medical Termination of Pregnancy Act 1971, 96
Administration system (*see* Public administration)
   district administration (*see* District administration)
Adult franchise
   universal, 110, 111, 120
Age, 13-17, 141
   age and monthly income, 16
   age group, 15
   place of birth, 16-17
   place of birth and choosing career, 17
   place of residence, 17
   upper age limit relaxable for various categories, 13-15
Agriculture
   agricultural land ceiling, 129-30, 132, 140
   agricultural technology, advanced, 129
   Green Revolution, 129
All India Services, 6, 7, 28, 29, 37
Andhra Pradesh, 60
Armed Forces Head Quarters Civil Services (Assistant Civil Staff Officers' Grade), 8
Arunachal Pradesh, 129
Assam, 35, 60
Assignments
   constant changes in, 136

Atrocities against women, 80
Attitude (s)
   education and, 80-81
   towards social change, 137-39
   towards women, 47, 79, 80-81
Authority
   rational-legal authority, 2-3
Autonomy, 136

Backward classes, 141
Bedi, Kiran, 46
Bengal, 60
Bhambhri, 15
Blunt, 6
Boys
   preferential treatment to, 73-74
Brahmins, 19, 20, 87
British Civil Service, 48
Buddhism, 23
Bureaucracy, 2-5, 6, 12, 130
   bureaucratic theory, 2-3
   characteristics of as enumerated by Max Weber, 3-4
   characteristics of as tabulated by Richard H Hall, 4-5
   definition of, 3-5
   Indian, 12, 45
   modern, 4
   socio-economic background of, 13

Career
   career importance, 41
   career importance in family, 41
   choosing of, 40-41
Caste system (Casteism), 59, 63, 102, 103, 137, 138
   Backward Community (BC), 18, 19, 20, 22
   caste and head of family, 20

discrimination of, 59, 135
drag on development and progress, 87
family type and, 33
Forward Community (FC), 18, 19, 20, 42, 134
lower castes, 134
Most Backward Community (MBC), 18, 19, 20, 22
Other Community (OC), 18, 19, 20, 22
Scheduled Castes (SC), 18, 19, 20, 21, 22, 134
Scheduled Tribes (ST), 18, 19, 21, 22, 134
suffered due to discrimination of, 59
traditional custom, 21-23
Central Secretariat Service (Section Officers' Grade), 7
Central Services, 6
Centre-States relations, 125
Chakiliars, 19
Chaturvedi, Geetha, 15, 38, 49, 85, 117, 129
Chettiars, 19
Children
care of, 66-68, 136: family type and, 68
child-marriage, 93, 137
family type and care of, 66-68, 136
handicapped, 66
help to, 68: family type and, 68
number of, 66
position of, 66
Christianity, 23
Christians, 18, 24, 25, 56, 57, 58, 83
Cochin Christian Succession Act 1921, 83
Travancore Christian Succession Act 1916, 83
Cinema, 100
Civil servants, 1, 51-53, 55, 61
allotment of specific tasks, 115-16, 120
efficiency of, 51, 52-53, 61
politicisation of, 2
promotions of, 113, 114, 120
right to strike, 116-17, 139
role of, 1

"statesman in disguise", term, 52
Civil service, 1, 6-10, 13
efficiency of, 113
examinations, 27
higher civil service in developmental activities, role of, 9-10
in India, 6-8
origin of, 5
recommendations of women to join, 61-62
recruitment in, 115, 116, 120
representation in, 113-15, 120, 143
term, 6
women in, 8-9
Cochin Christian Succession Act, 1921, 83
Competitive examination, 6
Cornwallis, Lord, 6
Corruption, 55
Crime against women, 141-42
Crozier, Michael, 5
Culture
cultural tradition of Tamil Nadu, 23
Hindu cultural traits, 32, 58
socio-cultural needs, 123
traditional custom, 21-23, 25, 56
Customs Appraisers' Service, 8

de Gournay, Vincent, 2
Delhi and Andaman & Nicobar Islands Police Service, 8
Democracy, 107, 108, 110, 119, 120, 139
best system, 108, 109
proportional representation, 108-10
socialism incompatible with, 112
two party system, 110-12
universal adult franchise, 110, 111, 120
unsuitable system, 108, 109
Didda, 45
Discrimination, 9, 59, 83, 96, 102, 135, 142
caste, 59, 135
language, 59-61, 135
religion, 59, 135
sex, 34, 58, 63, 135
District administration
collector, 9, 10
local resources for local needs, 10

Index

self-governing institutions of local bodies, 10
sub-divisional system, 10
sub-divisional magistrates, 10
uniform system of, planning of, 9
Domestic responsibilities (domestic domain) (domestic front) household responsibilities to, 65-78, 136-37
  authority in, 104
  neglect of home and working women, 71-72
  recognition of authority in, 101-02
  role at home, 66-78
Dowry, 80, 102, 103, 137, 138
  Dowry Prohibition Act 1961, 86
  Dowry Prohibition (Amendment) Act 1986, 86
  helps newly wed, 85
  lowers status of women, 85-87

ECOs, 14
Eating
  tradition of females eating after male members, 72-73, 137
Economy
  economic development, 123-32
  economic independency, 101, 102, 104, 139
  economic needs, 123
  mixed economy, 124, 132
  perspective on economic development, 140
  public sector in development, 127-28
  socio-economic background, 134-35
Education, 42, 93-95, 98, 103, 138, 140-41
  academic qualifications of respondents, 37-40
  attitudes and, 80-81
  co-education, 95, 139
  exclusive courses of study, 95
  fathers' qualification, 39, 42
  higher, 33
  husbands' qualifications, 38
  importance of, 94-95
  medium of instruction, 40, 42
  mothers' qualifications, 39, 42
  place of college studies, 40
  qualifications, 37-40, 93-94
  social attitude to girl's education, 94-95
  university education, 12, 134-35
Elections
  should not contest elections, 119
  universal adult franchise, 110, 111, 120
Elite services
  women in, 12-13
Emancipation, 140-43
Employment, 100
  opportunities, 35
Entertainment
  friends and guests, 137
  spending leisure time, 75
  time to entertain guest and relatives, 74-75
  traditional varieties of, 23
Equality, 103, 104
  treatment of men and women as equals, 81-85: men and women should have equal rights to property, 82-85
Everett, Jana, 20, 39
Examinations
  career oriented, 140
  competitive, 6
  Higher Civil Service examination, 8
Executives (executors), 55, 63, 72-73, 125, 129, 132, 137
Exploitation, 137

Family, 65-78
  care of children and, 66-68, 76
  care of sick and, 71
  caste and, 33
  cooking and serving and, 70, 76
  head of family, 34-36
  head of family and, 33
  help to children and, 68
  joint family (ies), 32, 33, 35, 67, 68, 69, 70, 71, 104: nuclearisation of, 104
  nuclear family, 32, 33, 42, 67, 68, 69, 70, 71, 76, 91-92, 103, 134
  purchase of grocery and, 69, 76
  status within their families, 136-37
  type of, 32-33

Fatalism, 98, 103
Fate
 belief in, 98
Festivals, 23
Fiscal federalism, 125-26, 132
Forward Community (FC) (Forward Castes), 18, 19, 20, 42, 134
 Brahmins, 19, 20, 87
 Chettiars, 19
 Gounders, 19
 Mudaliars, 19
 Vellalas, 19
Friedrich, 4

Gandhi, Mahatma
 feminise politics, 121
 women's oppression nearly universal, 120-21
 views of, 120-21
Garos, 35
Gavrou, Hannah, 48
Gender sensitisation programmes, 141
Goa, 83
God
 belief in, 97, 103, 139
Goode, William, J, 104
Gounders, 19
Green Revolution, 129 (see also Agriculture)
Guests and relatives
 time to entertain, 74-75
Gujarat
 Suicide Enquiry Committee, 93
Gupta, Prabhavati, 45

Hall, Richard H,
 characteristics of bureaucracy by, 4
Hastings, Warren, 6, 9
Heady, 4
Hierarchy, 4
Higher Civil Service
 examination, 8
Hindu culture, 32, 58
Hindus, 24, 25, 42, 56, 57, 58, 90, 134
Hinduism, 23, 24
Human rights, 141

Indian Administrative Service (IAS), 6, 7, 9, 10, 28, 29, 30, 37, 39, 42, 134
 IAS (recruitment) rules 1954, 8

number of women recruitment each year, 46
Indian Audit and Accounts Service, 7
Indian Civil Accounts Service, 7
Indian Civil Service (ICS), 6, 29
 Indian Civil Service Act 1861, 6
Indian Customs and Central Excise Service, 7
Indian Defence Accounts Service, 7
Indian Defence Estates Service, 7
Indian federation, 125
Indian Foreign Service (IFS), 7, 8, 9
Indian Information Service (Junior Grade), 7
Indian Ordinance Factories Service (Assistant Manager, Non Technical), 7
Indian P&T Accounts and Finance Service, 7
Indian Police Service (IPS), 6, 7, 8, 28, 29, 30, 42, 46, 134
Indian Police Service (recruitment) rules, 8
Indian Post Service, 7
Indian Railway Accounts Service, 7
Indian Railway Personnel Service, 7
Indian Revenue Service, 7
Indian Succession Act, 83 (see also Succession)
Industry (ies)
 heavy industries, 126, 132
 industrial development in India, 126-27
 Industrial Revolution in Europe, 46
 industrial towns: Bhilai, Jamshedpur, Ranchi, Renukoot, Rourkela, 126
 industrialisation, 126
 industrially advanced countries: France, Germany, Italy, Japan, UK, USA, USSR, 126
 large-scale, 126, 140
 small-scale, 126-27, 132, 140
Infanticide, female, 19
International Women's Decade, 79
Islam, 23

Jainism, 23
Javahir Devi, 46
Jeffreys, Margot, 48

Index

Job satisfaction, 48-50
   and reasons for taking job, 50
Judicial system (Judiciary), 112-13, 114, 120, 139

Kapadia, 88
Karnataka, 60
Kerala, 35, 60, 83
Khasis, 35
Kshatriyas (Warriors), 20, 87
Kumaradeve, 46

Lakshadweep, 35
Land
   agricultural land ceiling, 129-30, 132, 140
   urban property ceiling, 128-29, 132, 140
Language, 25-28, 63, 125
   daily newspaper respondents read, 28
   discrimination of, 135
   inter language rivalries, 60
   languages: Hindi, Kashmiri, Malayalam, Marathi, Tamil, Telugu, Urdu, 134
   medium of instruction in college, 27
   medium of instruction in school, 27
   mother tongue, 26-27
   recognised 15 languages, 26
   suffered due to discrimination of, 59-61
Litwak, 4

Macaulay, Lord, 60
Magazines
   types of magazines read by women, 75-76
Male
   colleagues, difficulty in working with, 56-57
   subordinates, difficulty in working with, 57-58
   superiors, difficulty in working with, 55-56
Malhotra, Anna, 8
Marriage, 94, 102
   age of, 92-93
   arranged marriage, 36, 37, 90-91, 103
   child marriage, 93, 137
   cross-cousin marriage, 90
   inter-caste marriage, 36, 86, 87-88, 103
   Inter-religious marriage, 36
   love marriage, 37, 42, 88-90, 103
   marital status and type of marriage, 34, 36-37: divorcees, married, single, 34
   matrilineal system, 34-35
   Special Marriage Act 1954, 89, 92
   type of, 34, 36-37
   widow's marriage, 83, 92, 103
Media (Mass media)
   degrading (lower) image of women in, 98-100, 103
   exploitation of image by, 137, 139
   freedom of, 118-121
   print media, 99
Meghalaya, 35, 129
Merton, Robert, 4, 5
Mizoram, 129
Moplahs (Muslims), 35
Morality (Moral), 103, 109
   moral life and religion, 97
Motherhood, 65-78 (*passim*)
Mudaliars, 19
Mukerji, D P, 130
Muslims, 18, 24, 25, 35, 56, 57, 58
Myrdal, Gunnar, 123

Nagaland, 129
Nairs, 35
National Academy of Administration, Mussoorie, 29
National Committee on the Status of Women in India, 84
National integration, 103
   intercaste marriage helps in, 87-88 (*see also* Marriage)
Nayanika, 45
Newspapers
   whether read only national or both local and national, 76
North-eastern, 35

O'Malley, 6

Pallars, 19
Panicker, Sardar, 5
Parayars, 19
Parliament
　reservation of seats in, 118, 119
Parsees, 83
Parsons, 4
Pending files, 53-55
　experience and, 54
　view on taking, 54
Planning, 121, 130-31
　decentralisation of, 132, 140
　Planning Commission, 131
Police
　women in (women officers), 142
Political system, 120
　characteristics, 106-07
　features, general, 106-07
　opinion about, 139-40
　term, 106
　two party system, 110-12
Politics
　active participation in, 101, 102, 104, 107, 118, 139
　women unsuitable for, 117
Pondicherry Civil Service, 8
Posts of Assistant Commandant in Central Industrial Security Force, 7
Posts of Assistant Security Officer in Railways Protection Force, 7
Posts of Deputy Superintendent of Police in the Central Bureau of Investigation, 8
Posts of respondents, 28-30
　posts of women administrators, 29
　posts of women administrators and occupation of their husbands, 29-30
　posts of women administrators and occupation of their mothers, 30
　posts of women administrators and their fathers occupation, 30
Poverty, 100, 123-24
　exploitation of poor women, 100
Press
　freedom of, 118 (*see also* Mass media)
Private sector
　women in, 12
Property
　inheritance of, 102
　men and women should have equal right to, 82-85
　urban property ceiling, 128-29
Prostitution, 100, 103, 137, 139
　commercialisation of, 100
　legislation, 103, 139
　to be legalised, 100
Public administration (Public administrative system) (Administrative system)
　fourth organ of government, 1
　place in, 139-40
　policy-making, 1-2
　political interference, 2
　role of, 1
Public sector (Public enterprises), 132, 140
　growth of public sectors check monopolies, 128
　investments, 127-28
　role in development, 127-28

Race, 102, 125
Railway Board Secretariat Service (Section Officers' Grade), 8
Recruitment, 139
Red-tapism, 55
Relatives and guests
　time to entertain, 74-75
Religion, 23-25, 63, 102, 103, 125, 139
　and difficulty in working with male colleagues, 57
　and difficulty in working with male superiors, 56
　and family type of women administrators, 24-25
　discrimination of, 59, 135
　moral life and, 97
　of women administrators, 24
　suffered due to discrimination of, 59
　traditional customs, 25
Representation in administration (civil services), 141, 143
　equal from all social and economic classes, 139
　proportional of minorities, 139
Reservation, 103, 139, 140, 143

Index

in education and jobs uplift social status, 95
in legislature, 120
in Parliament, 118, 119
Revenue
  administration, 6
  operations, 10
Rights, 141
  Constitutional and legal rights, 104, 139
  fundamental rights, 129, 132, 140
  neutralisation of, 102-03

SSCOs, 14
Sahai, 12
Scheduled Castes and Scheduled Tribes (SC & ST), 9, 134, 141
Self-reliance, 126
Service (in service), 47-63
  assignments, constant changes in, 136
  caste, suffered due to discrimination of, 59
  efficiency, frequent transfer affects, 61
  experiences in, unpleasant, 61, 135
  job satisfaction, 48-50, 52, 53, 62
  job satisfaction vs recommendation of women administrators to service, 62
  male colleagues, difficulty in working with, 56-57
  male colleagues, religion and difficulty in working with, 57
  male subordinates, difficulty in working with, 57-58
  male superiors, difficulty in working with, 55-56
  pending files, 53-55: experience and, 54; views on taking, 54
  reasons for taking job, 48, 50
  religion, suffered due to discrimination of, 59
  sex, suffered due to discrimination of, 58
  status at office, 135-36
  superiors, religion and difficulty in working with male, 56
  superiors, suggestions to, 55
  transfers, frequent, 61, 135
  transfers, routine, 136
  unpleasant experience, 61, 135
  work after office hours, 52-53
  workload, 50-52
Sex, 102
  discrimination, 58, 63
  sex determination, 104, 139 tests, 79, 100-01
  suffered due to discrimination of, 58
Sick
  care of, 70-71
Sikhism, 23
Sikhs, 18
Singh, Y., 112, 123
Social sector
  social attitude to girl's education, 94-95
  social awareness, 140
  social change, attitude towards, 137-39
  social change, need for, 80
  social inequalities faced, 139
  social inequality of men and women, 104
  social justice, 95, 105
  social prestige, 94-95
  social reforms, 55
  social status, 94, 95
  socially backward communities, 19
  socio-cultural needs, 123
  socio-economic background, 134-35
Socialism, 111, 112, 120, 139
  incompatible with democracy, 112
Srinivas, 18
States Reorganisation Commission (SRC), 59
Status of women (*see* Women)
"Stridhanam", 83
Strike
  right to, 116
Succession
  Cochin Christian Succession Act 1921, 83
  Indian Succession Act, 83
  Travancore Christian Succession Act 1916, 83
Sudras (Cultivators and Menials), 20, 87
Sugandha, 45
Suicide

among young married women, 93
Suicide Enquiry Committee, 93
Superiors
  difficulty in working with male superiors, 55-56
  suggestions, to, 55

Tamil Nadu, 13, 18, 19, 23, 34, 42, 60, 67, 69, 76, 77, 134, 143
Taxation
  heavy taxation, 130, 132: policy, 140
  progressive tax system, 124-25, 132
Taub, Richard P., 20, 37, 134
Thevars, 19
Thiyars, 35
Traditional
  attitude towards women, 47
  patriarchal values, 99
  values, 72-73
Transfer (s), 61, 135, 136
  frequent transfers effect efficiency, 61
Travancore Christian Succession Act 1916, 83
Tribal women, 20

UPSC (Union Public Service Commission), 9, 13, 27, 28, 40, 140, 143
Udy, 4
Unemployment, 95, 137, 140
Untouchability, 21
  untouchables, 19
Urban
  land ceiling, 132, 140
  property ceiling, 128-29

Vaisyas (Land holders and Merchants), 20, 87
Vellalas, 19
Vijayabhattarika, 45
Weber, Max, 2, 3-4

characteristics of bureaucracy enumerated by (Weberian bureaucracy), 3-4
definition of bureaucracy by, 3-4
Widow
  remarriage of, 83, 92, 103
Women
  All India Women's Conference, Phalton (23rd February 1955), 9
  atrocities against, 80
  attitude towards, 47, 79, 80-81
  domestic responsibilities (domestic domain), 65-78 (see also Domestic responsibilities)
  dowry (see Dowry)
  family for, 65-78 (see also Family)
  motherhood, 65-78 (passim)
  privileges, 19
  programmes for welfare of, 10
  role models, 141
  status, 85-87, 93, 100, 101-02, 104, 141, 143
    at office, 135-36
    dowry lowers status, 85-87
    National Committee on the Status of Women in India, 84
    report of committees on status of, 47
    views regarding elevation, 101-02
    within their families, 136-37
  traditional attitude towards, 47
  university education to, 12, 134-35
Work (see also Service)
  after office hours, 52-53
  work experience, 31, 51
  income of women administrators and their husbands' income, 31
  monthly income of respondents, 31
  workload, 50-53

Zweig, 48